Studies in applied regional science

This series in applied regional, urban and
environmental analysis aims to provide
regional scientists with a set of adequate tools
for empirical regional analysis and for practical regional planning problems. The major
emphasis in this series will be upon the
applicability of theories and methods in the
field of regional science; these will be presented in a form which can be readily used
by practitioners. Both new applications of
existing knowledge and newly developed ideas
will be published in the series.

D1705403

Studies in applied regional science Vol. 4

Locational behavior in manufacturing industries

William R. Latham III
University of Delaware

Martinus Nijhoff Social Sciences Division
Leiden 1976

ISBN 90 207 0638 1

Photoset in Malta by Interprint (Malta) Ltd.

Printed in the Netherlands

To Sal

Preface

The research incorporated in this monograph was initially undertaken as part of a Ph.D. dissertation submitted to the University of Illinois in 1973. Revisions were accomplished at the University of Delaware.

I want to gratefully acknowledge the assistance of Hugh O. Nourse who suggested the investigation, Paul Chouinard who ably and accurately translated verbal instructions into computer programmes, and Harold F. Williamson, Jr. and Peter Nijkamp who commented at length on earlier drafts of the manuscript. Rapid and accurate typing of several drafts of the manuscript and valuable editorial assistance were provided by my wife, Sally M. Latham.

Contents

List of tables

1. Introduction

The objective of this investigation is the extension of empirically validated knowledge of the determinants of the location of economic activity. Hopefully, the investigation yields information useful to policy makers concerned with such locations. The author believes that, in order to formulate effective policies with respect to the location of economic activities, the nature of locational decisions must be understood. The need for such understanding is detailed briefly in the following section of this Chapter. The theoretical understanding which forms the basis for this investigation is the classical or Weberian industrial location theory which is outlined below in this Chapter. This theory holds that locations for economic activities are determined primarily by certain factors of location, such as the location of markets, resources, labor supplies and other factors often called agglomerative economies.

Location in this investigation is considered primarily in terms of geographic associations between economic activities, i.e. the simultaneous occurrence of different economic activities in the same geographic regions. From a policy point of view such associations are particularly important because, at any point in time, the set of economic activities in each region is fixed, and policies that affect location affect the geographic association of these activities. Therefore an understanding of the determinants of geographic association can be helpful to policy makers. A basic hypothesis of this investigation, and one which appears to be supported in the following chapters, is that the classical factors of location (markets, resources, labor and agglomerative economies) are important in explaining the geographic associations of some economic activities.

A following section of this chapter justifies the concentration of this investigation on manufacturing industries rather than on all economic activity primarily because these are the activities most likely to be influenced by policy makers. Without neglecting other factors, which are found to be important for some industries, the investigation also focuses on agglomerative economies, as defined below, because they have been less well-understood than other factors of location in explaining geographic associations. In this study, agglomerative economies are subdivided into two distinct groups. One, which is found to be important for some industries, consists of those economies derived from potential savings on transportation costs on inputs or outputs obtained from or sold to other manufacturing industries. These economies are described in detail below in Chapter 3. The second subdivision of agglomerative economies, found to be more important for more industries than the first group, consists of those due to more generalized economies available in industrial concentrations. This second group of agglomerative economies is also discussed below and detailed in Chapter 5.

Previous work in this area, especially that of Richter [41] and Streit [47], was limited in both geographic scope and industrial detail. Below and in Chapter 2 are detailed reasons for believing that both the broader geographic scope and greater industrial detail used in this study represent significant improvements in this type of analysis. Additional contributions of this investigation in comparison with previous investigations of the impact of agglomerative economies on industrial location include the utilization of measures of other factors of location in the analysis (see Chapter 5) and improvements in both the measure of geographic association (see Chapter 4) and the measure of each factor (see Chapters 3 and 5).

The next section of this chapter provides an indication of the importance of industrial location analysis for policy makers. Following sections outline the theoretical basis for the analysis and describe, in particular, the agglomerative economies referred to above.

THE NEED FOR INDUSTRIAL LOCATION ANALYSIS

The importance of understanding the forces which cause firms to locate geographically within the U.S. as they do arises from at least three sources. 1. Decision makers for firms have a need to know which is the optimal location for an anticipated new facility or expansion. 2. Communities need to know which industries can and should be attracted to yield maximum benefits to the community from given resources. 3. Federal and state resources devoted to area development should be used as efficiently as possible.[1] That firms actively seek locations which are, in some sense, optimal is attested by the prosperity of consultants and firms offering advice on site selection. Because capital facilities of industrial firms are most commonly immobile after their initial location has been chosen, firms pay a penalty for suboptimal location over a long period of time and are therefore highly motivated to seek optimal locations. The interest of communities in industrial location can be observed through the actions of their representative bodies and appointed agencies. Efforts to attract industries have spawned regional planning agencies and have produced industrial parks, zoning laws, and local tax benefits for individual firms and industries [6]. The involvement of the federal government in industrial location is evidenced by the activities of the Economic Development Administration and its publications, such as the one entitled *How to Improve Your Community by Attracting New Industry* [55].[2]

The incomplete knowledge of factors influencing location on the part of many of those who are practicing industrial location is obvious in documents such as the one referred to above and in statements such as the following: 'Consumption [of rubber] is many times production [in the area], which is sufficient reason for considering a plant in the area to meet local requirements' [30: XIX–85]. The development of better empirical analysis, such as this study attempts, will hopefully increase the sophistication of the practitioners in ways that will contribute to greater economic stability as more firms are able to choose profitable locations and to more efficient use of community resources devoted to community development.

CONCENTRATION ON DISAGGREGATED MANUFACTURING ACTIVITY

All economic activity may be subdivided or categorized in various ways. One division often used in introductory economics courses places activities either in households or firms. This study deals only with activities undertaken by firms and generally aggregates the firms into industries. All the industries in the economy can then be categorized as belonging to one of three main industry groups which may be called 1. primary resource extractors, 2. manufacturers and 3. services (including financial institutions). Reasons for making manufacturing industries the exclusive subject of this study are detailed in the following paragraphs.

First, these industries account for a very large proportion of industrial activity in the U.S., and analysis of manufacturing therefore provides information about a primary sector of U.S. industry. While the economic principles of location are generalizable to economic activity in any industrial sector there may be some advantage in examining a particular sector whose common characteristics permit a more specific analysis that is also possibly more useful for policy purposes. Instead of attempting to investigate empirically the whole range of industrial economic activity from natural resource extraction through final distribution, focusing on the processes that we call manfacturing industry may permit a richer analysis of this more limited set of activities.

Second, manufacturing has been considered by many to be the most important of the 'basic' activities of regions and to the extent that regional growth and development depend upon such 'basic' activities 'knowledge of the factors determining the location of manufacturing establishments is essential' [20: 1].[3] The merits of the export base theory of regional growth have been and continue to be debated. The viability of the concept of the export base lies primarily in the fact that an undeniable element of truth lies in the idea that expanded exports produce expanded regional income. While more recently the possibility of services being an 'export' industry has been recognized, and primary resources have traditionally been exported, those interested in consciously altering the export base of underdeveloped regions have continued to concentrate their attention on attracting manufacturing industries to these areas. This is largely because firms in manufacturing industries have more freedom in choosing their locations than do firms in the other industrial sectors. Firms in sectors such as agriculture, livestock, forestry and fishing products, and mining have considerably less choice in locating than most manufacturing firms have. The former are often tied to natural resources to a considerable degree and would thus be less likely to locate in response to other economic factors such as the agglomerative economies discussed below. Location for extractive firms is a matter of choosing which resource sites to exploit. Similarly, firms in construction, transportation, and financial and other services industries also have less locational choice than do manufacturing firms. The former are usually closely tied to large populations and large markets and are less likely to illustrate the type of locational behavior of interest in this study. Intraregional location may be a more relevant consideration than interregional location for these firms. While it is true that among both manufacturing and service industries one will find those whose locations are determined primarily by the location of populations, or other markets, by the location of essential resources, and by the location of important agglomerative economies, the two groups, in the aggregate, are significantly different in their locational behaviors. Manufacturing industries can and frequently do choose nonurban and even completely undeveloped locations. Service industries are almost always dependent upon the prior existence of a market for their products, and must locate in proximity to the existing market because of transportation costs for their outputs or agglomerative economies available only in large places. This contention that the locational characteristics of services and manufacturing industries are significantly different could be put to a statistical test but such a test is beyond the scope of the present study. In addition the separation of services from manufacturing industries is a well-established practice based upon empirical relationships.[4]

There are no doubt exceptions to the above generalizations in all sectors but, on balance, manufacturing firms would seem to be more likely to exemplify locational decision-making in response to factors such as the particular agglomerative economies of most interest in this study, as defined below, than would firms in other sectors. The study recognizes that ties to firms in the resource extractive and service sectors may also be important locational forces for many manufacturing industries. These are dealt with in an aggregative way as resource and market orientations as described below and in Chapter 3 and provide the basis for a further subdivision of the manufacturing sector into primary resource users, primary suppliers of final demand and those intermediate between these two classes. Additional factors contributing to the choice of only manufacturing industries include a desire to limit the scope of the study to one that was feasible with the time and resources available to the author and the fact that the locational data, described in Chapter 2, are available only for manufacturing industries.

THE LOCATION OF ECONOMIC ACTIVITY

The factors which influence the locational decisions of firms can generally be divided into those of a noneconomic nature and those primarily economic in nature. The noneconomic factors include political pressure, the social, cultural and physical amenities of various locations, the personal pre-ferences of decision makers, and all other factors which vary from one geographic location to another but do not affect the costs of production or distribution of the firm's product. The importance of such factors in deter-mining the locations of firms has been well documented.[5] The effects of these noneconomic factors on locational decisions are difficult to subject to precise, quantitative analysis, however, and will not be dealt with explicitly in this study. This is not meant to imply that noneconomic factors cannot be used in locational analysis because they are difficult to quantify. In fact some, such as mean temperature, rainfall and number of university students, are subject to precise measurement. Others, such as presence or absence of a seashore, symphony orchestra or airport can be introduced through a variety of techniques including attribute scaling and dummy variables in regression analysis. Even if these factors are not introduced directly into the formal analysis they may be used indirectly. In this study such factors are omitted because of the aggregate nature of the analysis. They are more readily incorporated into analyses of individual regions or individual industries.

The particular geographic dispersion of industrial firms observed at any given time may be viewed as the product of an historical process that may have been economically determined to a great extent in its development.[6] Because the economic forces which dictated present industrial locations may no longer be operative, only inertia and the present costs of relocating can explain why many firms remain non-optimally located.[7] Their present locations are thus not the product of existing economic factors, but of technological and other noneconomic factors. Wilfred Smith stated this more colorfully as follows:

The industrial landscape is a mosaic of infinite variety, made up of repetitive patterns adjusted to this or that condition, embodying relics of archaic distributions, the reasons for whose original establishments have passed away, but which continue to operate by the momentum of an established business and by the practice of special economies which permit their survival ... [43: 20].

To perform a meaningful analysis based on economic factors alone and without extensive historical data, it must be assumed that a significant proportion of firms are presently located as they are because of economic factors still in effect. This assumption seems justified so long as the economy is not changing radically at a rapid rate. According to accepted theory, firms whose locations are not economically 'best' and which are consequently less profitable than they might be, will, in the long run, relocate or cease to operate. At any given time in a slowly changing economy the preponderance of observed firms can be assumed to be, in some sense, located primarily in accordance with economic principles [44: 3]. For the above reasons it will be assumed for the remainder of this study that current economic factors are of sufficient importance to substantially affect present locations.

The factors of location approach
The location of economic activities in space can be approached from a general equilibrium point of view with decisions regarding prices, outputs, inputs, production, and location interacting to produce an optimal solution.[8] The implementation of such an analysis for the entire U.S. economy is not feasible with current data and methodology, however. Fortunately, the sequential nature of location decisions and their irrevocable nature in the short run, implicit in the preceding discussion, permit a useful and meaningful analysis of the locational decisions of individual firms with the location of all other activities considered to be fixed. The approach of the present study is to examine data regarding industrial locations in the form of geographic associations at a specific point in time in such a way that probable factors influencing those associations can be deduced. It is understood throughout that firms seek maximum profit locations and that such locations can be found only with knowledge of the spatial variations in revenues and costs for each firm. The present study does not consider cost or revenue functions explicitly, but rather uses empirical data to categorize firms in various industries as having found maximum profit locations which correspond to certain 'location factors.'

Lists of potential location factors vary considerably in both number and type of factors considered.[9] All the various possible economic factors can be fitted into simplifying schemes. The simple categorization used in this study is based on Isard's modern Weberian framework [22: 577]. Weber originally emphasized transport costs as the most important locational factor and identified labor costs and agglomerative economies as other major industrial location factors [37]. Isard expanded Weber's framework to account for subsequent additions to, and factor classifications in, the theory of industrial location. The modern Weberian framework retains transport cost differentials as the major determinant of location.

For any firm different locations entail differentials in transport costs 1. on inputs, including raw materials, and 2. on outputs, including those sold to final consumers. Some inputs, such as the unique benefits available in one urban area, are not transportable and thus can be considered to have infinitely high transport costs. In this way the agglomerative economies known as urbanization economies can be considered as forms of transport cost economies. Similarly, when large regions are considered, the inter-regional transportation cost for labor inputs is extremely high in the short run and thus labor costs as a factor of location can also be considered to be another form of transport costs. Even though all factors can be reduced to a form of transport cost, it is useful to distinguish certain types of transport costs as important locational factors and to identify industries for which one factor dominates all others as being 'oriented' to that factor.

This notion of 'orientation' of industries to various factors has persisted since the earliest discussions of industrial location. While the discussants have usually recognized that firms are, at least theoretically, maximum-profit oriented, continued discussion of industrial orientation has been encouraged by the empirical fact that the maximum-profit location for many firms coincides with that which would be dictated by consideration of only a single factor. Lösch is among those who have reminded us that 'concepts like production orientation or transport orientation merely describe a location; they do not explain it' [31: 377].[10] Klaassen has also pointed out that concepts such as labor orientation imply that substitution possibilities among inputs are not great [25b: 35]. In fact many discussions of orientation implicitly assume fixed input proportions in production. While this is unjustifiable for many industries, in the short run firms may regard productive technologies as severly limited. In addition, if revenues and all other costs are roughly equal spatially, lower costs for any single input will make the low cost sites more attractive even if substitution possibilities are great. Thus the concept of orientation remains useful and meaningful in describing the locational behavior of some firms.

In this study market, material, labor and agglomerative economy orientations are considered. Each of these is, in reality, a form of transport orientation as was indicated above. Any other factor influencing either the production or distribution of a product could be singled out for considera-tion as well, but those chosen are among the ones most commonly con-sidered.[11]

It should be noted that not all industries will have an identifiable orientation in some classification schemes. Based on 1954 data, Lichtenberg reported that 12.5% of manufacturing employment in the U.S. was in industries
whose orientation could not be neatly classified and, as noted above,
another 13.9% was in industries whose original orientations were no longer
economically optimal and thus whose locations could be attributed only to
inertia [29: 39].

When the need to reduce transport costs for raw materials obtained from
primary resource extractors dominates all other considerations, a firm
locating near these resource extractors may be identified as material
oriented. Location near final demand (consumers of a firm's final products)
in order to reduce transportation costs for distribution may identify the
firm as being market oriented. Location near input suppliers other than
primary resource extractors or near output purchasers other than final
consumers may identify the firm as agglomerative economy oriented as
discussed further in the following section. Industries for whom labor cost
differentials are the dominant locational factor may be identified as labor
oriented.

Labor orientation differs from market, material or agglomerative orientation in one fundamental respect. While firms may vary either distribution costs or transport costs on inputs by locating closer or farther from
their markets or input suppliers, reductions in labor costs are usually
possible only by locating at low-cost labor markets.[12] This is because, as
noted above, the interregional transportation cost for labor is extremely
high in the short run when the regions considered are large. The method
of identifying each of these orientations and the particular industries so
identified are discussed in Chapter 3.

A practical problem which has not been resolved in the present study is
related to the fact that factors of location are usually thought of as having a
site which lies within a particular region. Advantages may be obtained by a
firm being near to these sites, even if the firm does not locate in the region
that contains the site of the factor. Thus a region may have a significant
locational advantage for firms in some industry even though it is not the site
of any of the industry's factors. In such a case one would have to count as a
locational factor for the region the spillover effects from other regions.
From the point of view of the firm such factors can be especially important
if the costs of obtaining the services of the factor are lower in adjacent
regions than in the region where the factor is located. For example the
benefits of a low cost natural resource may be obtained in adjacent regions
which do not bear any of the taxation burden used to maintain the availability of the resource. In the present study these spillover effects are
assumed to be of a small enough magnitude as not to alter substantially the
results achieved when they are ignored.

The next section elaborates on agglomerative economies because they are of most interest in the present study for the reasons outlined above.

Agglomerative economies as location factors
The category of agglomerative economies as a location factor has been expanded and refined considerably since Weber. It has also been confused and erroneously truncated in a number of ways. The following paragraphs will hopefully clarify this category of location factors and will specify precisely the particular agglomerative economies of major interest in this study.

Agglomerative economies almost always arise from external economies of areal concentration.[13] In order to produce areal concentrations, these external economies must be geographically immobile in the sense that they must be available only to a firm in geographic proximity to their source.[14] These economies may be subdivided into four groups:
1. Those internal to the firm.
2. Those external to the firm but internal to the industry (also known as localization economies; includes most of Weber's agglomerative economies [57]; with (3) and (4), constitutes part of Isard's spatial juxtaposition economies [22].)
3. Those external to the industry not attributable to transfers (known as generalized agglomerative economies in the present study; Hoover's urban concentration economies [17]; with (4), part of urbanization economies; with (2) and (4), part of Isard's spatial juxtaposition economies [22]; with (4), part of Stevens, Douglas and Neighbor's industrial complex economies [46]; part of economies producing Czamanski's urban orientation which also includes market orientation [8].)
4. Those external to the industry and attributable to transfers (known as agglomerative economies in the present study; with (3), part of urbanization economies; with (2) and (3), part of Isard's spatial juxtaposition economies [22]; with (3), part of Stevens, Douglas and Neighbor's industrial complex economies [46]; economies producing Czamanski's complementary orientation in part, and also that part of his geographic orientations not included with material orientations [8].)

The fourth group includes reductions in transport costs from the spatial juxtaposition of firms in different industries. When these cost reductions are on inputs from primary resource extractors they produce the material orientations referred to above. When the reduced transport costs are on outputs sold to final demand they produce the market orientations also referred to above. It is the reductions in transport costs on the inputs and outputs traded between manufacturing industries by spatial juxtaposition of firms in these industries that are the specific economies referred to in the remainder of this study as agglomerative economies.[15] The term would be equally applicable to economies arising from the spatial juxtaposition of a manufacturing firm and a services firm. The previously discussed focus on manufacturing industries unfortunately results in these agglomerative economies not being analyzed. However, this error of omission does not invalidate any of the findings regarding agglomerative economies among manufacturing industries. Measurement of these economies is discussed below in Chapters 3 and 4. Their impact on geographic associations of industries is explored in Chapter 5. An additional reason for concentrating on these agglomerative economies is because the first three groups identified above are clearly related to size or scale within the firm, industry, or collection of industries while agglomerative economies of the fourth are not. The author agrees with Chinitz, that 'we have been too prone to associate external economies and diseconomies with size' [7: 289]. (In Chapter 4 the effect of size on geographic association is considered, but the effect of size on agglomerative economies is not investigated.)

The third group of economies above can also produce spatial juxtapositions but they are not primarily to achieve transport cost reductions. These economies are referred to as generalized agglomerative economies and their effects are discussed below in Chapter 5.

A major objective of this study may now be stated. It is to quantify the extent to which the economies of the third and fourth groups may have influenced the locational pattern of manufacturing industries in the U.S., allowing for the effects of other factors of location.

The discussion in this chapter yields a model which may be stated verbally as follows: The location of the firms in an industry, as measured by their geographic associations with firms in other industries, is a function of the degree to which the industry is material, market, labor, or agglomerative economy oriented. Industries and their locational patterns may thus be distinguished on the basis of the relative weighting of these factors. The model above is estimated for a sample of manufacturing industries in Chapter 5 after developing appropriate measures for the independent variables in Chapter 3 and the dependent variable in Chapter 4. A major predecessor in this type of industrial location analysis was Richer [41], whose work would probably be placed by Stevens and Brackett among the 'nontheoretical attacks on agglomeration economies [that] fail to distinguish the basic components of these economies ...' [45: 12]. The present study has more clearly identified the basic components of agglomeration economies above, and has identified the particular components to be explored in this study, the agglomerative economies of the fourth group and the generalized agglomerative economies of the third group.

In previous studies of industrial location highly aggregated manufacturing industries were used. Richter [41] used 50 manufacturing industries from the 1958 Input-Output Study and Streit [47] used 26 industries in both France and West Germany. Richter recognized that one of the difficulties with his study was the heterogenous nature of many of the industries that he used [42: 19]. They included mostly two-digit and three-digit SIC industries; at this level of aggregation many effects may have been partially masked by aggregate figures and potentially significant relationships may have been completely obscured.[16] Richter had little choice at the time of his work because data on values of flows of goods and services between industries were not available at a more disaggregated level.

Isard and Langford proposed that 'it is necessary in general to have disaggregation at least at a 4-digit sector breakdown in order to avoid errors from grouping together establishments with product mixes that differ greatly' [23: 4]. Spiegelman [44] was able to use four-digit SIC's in his study but he only included 53 industries. A major strength of the present study is its use of four-digit SIC industries.

The present study has also expanded the geographic scope of the analysis from the 51 metropolitan areas considered by Richter to the entire U.S. The significance of this expansion is explained in Chapter 2.

OUTLINE OF FOLLOWING CHAPTERS

The preceding paragraphs give some indication of the critical importance of data in this type of industrial location analysis. The importance of the data base for such studies is of such magnitude that the bulk of Chapter 2 is devoted to describing and analyzing in considerable detail the data used to identify potential agglomerative economies and the data reflecting the geographic distributions of the industries after first carefully defining the regions upon which the study is based. Chapter 3 develops measures of the extent to which manufacturing industries may be considered to be footloose or oriented to one of the factors discussed above. There the specific method of identifying each type of orientation is detailed. Chapter 4 explores means of measuring agglomeration or spatial juxtaposition of industries. Chapter 5 then examines the impact which agglomerative economies have had on spatial juxtaposition in the U.S. economy. Bilateral relationships between industries are examined with the aid of multiple regression models using the measures developed in Chapters 3 and 4. Multilateral relationships are commented upon briefly in a section on industrial complexes. Chapter 6 summarizes the results of the study, states some conclusions that might reasonably be drawn from these results and indicates some potentially fruitful avenues for further research.

NOTES

1. See Hoover [18] pp. 241–300 for the role of public policy in location.
2. The '1961 International Site Selection Handbook' lists more than 11,000 organizations which are engaged in industrial development activities at local, area, state or national levels [20].
3. A recent commentary and bibliography on this point are provided in Braschler [5: 109–111].
4. See, for example, Perloff *et al.* [38: 677ff].
5. See Tiebout [49] for examples from surveys.
6. Location models which explicitly consider the dynamic and sequential nature of decision making are as yet highly abstract and require data unavailable at present. Dziewonski [12], for example, proposed utilizing a concept of socio-economic time-space.
7. Lichtenberg reported that in 1954, 13.9% of total manufacturing employment in the U.S. was in industries whose dominant locational factor was inertia [29:39]. Menchik observed that 'Manufacturing plants and other workplaces are generally highly immobile.... To [this reason] for the slow rate of spatial adjustment, we may add the familiar general causes of slow behavioral change – acquaintance with only the old practices, uncertainty about new behavior, and the money and psychic costs of change' [35: 154].
8. See Takayama and Judge [48] for a mathematical statement of an optimum.
9. See 'Master List of Location Factors' [20] for an exhaustive listing.
10. Pred went further and stated, 'there is no single touchstone capable of intelligibly and precisely explaining industrial concentration' [39: 132].
11. Orientations suggested by other authors include Klaassen's [25] demand and supply orientations, which are related to the market and material orientations used here, but include all output purchasers and input suppliers. The market and supply area analysis of the modern Weberian framework is similarly related to the orientations discussed in this study. The modern Weberian framework also expands Weber's labor cost differentials including differentials on power, water, and other processing costs in addition to labor [21: 133]. Labor is the only one of these given explicit consideration in this study. The others become part of the generalized agglomerative economies discussed below.
12. This applies to wage rates within normal ranges in the short run. The ability of firms to attract low-cost labor to their sites, especially if the offered wage is significantly higher than that available at labor's origin or if unemployment rates are high at the origin, is recognized.
13. Mishan stated that an 'essential feature of an external effect is that the effect produced is not a deliberate creation but an unintended or incidental by-product of some otherwise legitimate activity' [36: 2]. In the area of location theory this feature may be out of place because firms take purposeful action to take advantage of external economies that are only potential until they take action. Furthermore some of these potential external economies are consciously created by public or private agents.
14. As explained above, labor orientation is also produced by a geographically immobile economy.
15. In the preceding discussion of external economies no reference was made to a distinction between pecuniary and technological or real economies. With the exception of Bain, industrial location practitioners and theorists have not found the distinction necessary or useful [3: 57]. In addition it has been shown that any technological economy can be converted to a pecuniary one by appropriate pricing of inputs [58: 883].
16. The Standard Industrial Classification, SIC, system breaks all industries down into major industry groups which have a two-digit designation and subdivides each group into component major industries (three-digit designations) which are further subdivided into specific industries (four-digit designations). The system extends to the seven-digit level for some industries.

2. Description of the data base

Several advantages of the present study in comparison with previous related work are based upon the richness of the data used. The detail and relative completeness of the data permit a more precise analysis with more meaningful conclusions than has previously been possible.

This chapter describes the data base of the analysis. The system of geographic regions used is first presented. Then the regional data on industrial location are examined, and, finally, the aggregate industrial data used to identify possible agglomerative economies are described.

REGIONS USED

In determining the regions to be used for the spatial aspects of the present study, three criterial were considered most relevant. The first was that the regions should span the U.S. omitting no areas. Most manufacturing industries have historically tended to locate in or near major cities, especially in the 'manufacturing belt' extending from New York and New England west to Chicago and south to Baltimore. More recently, however, many new manufacturing establishments have located outside of major metropolitan areas. The dimensions of this movement out of the metropolitan areas are of interest to the residents and planners of both types of area and to all firms.

The geographic industry data used by Richter [41] came from only 54 of the 70 largest standard metropolitan statistical areas (SMSA's) in the U.S. and three whole states. In constructing his model of urban growth Czmanski [8] used industry data for 232 cities in the U.S. Both failed to provide information about non-SMSA areas. Streit [47] was able to use 30 regions for all of Germany and 90 for all of France in his analysis. Although the latter two sets of regions span entire countries, neither is really satisfactory for the analysis of industrial location because the regional boundaries in both cases are political rather than economic. Spiegelman [44] used 506 State Economic Areas spanning the U.S. These would have provided a finer grid than the set of regions finally selected, but State Economic Areas suffer from the requirement that no SEA extend beyond the political boundary of a single state.

A set of regions spanning the country is also desirable from a statistical point of view. The exclusion of data from certain areas could introduce bias if the characteristics of industries in these areas differed significantly from the characteristics of industries in included areas. For example, if a large proportion of the establishments in a particular industry are in excluded areas, spurious significant associations of that industry with others located only in included areas may be deduced from analysis of the data from included areas only. In addition, if only SMSA's are used it becomes much more difficult to separate the effects of generalized agglomerative economies from the agglomerative economies related to transfers of inputs and outputs.

Use of a system of regions completely spanning the country should provide additional distinct advantages over using only SMSA's. For some industries the size of establishments located in a region may be directly related to the population of the region. Because SMSA's are centers of large populations, only the larger establishments in such industries would enter into any analysis utilizing only SMSA's. Extrapolation to non-SMSA areas in such cases would be hazardous. Furthermore, one hypothesis tested in the present study states that the level of output of an industry in a region affects its locational attraction for firms in different industries. The use of a set of areas spanning the U.S., including areas outside SMSA's, increases the range of outputs observed for many industries and therefore makes the test more meaningful.

The second criterion used in selecting a set of regions was the availability of data. Industry output and employment data of the type desired (described below) are available for a very limited number of geographic areas. Less desirable, but acceptable data of the type used by Richter for part of his analysis is available for all of the counties and independent cities in the U.S. It was decided that the regions should be based on counties in order to take advantage of the availability of highly disaggregated employment data for all counties.

The final criterion influencing the selection of regions was that use of the regions should have some economic meaning. For this reason, single counties defined by political boundaries were not used as regions. Instead, counties were aggregated into economically meaningful regions. The 34 independent cities in Virginia; the independent cities of St. Louis, Missouri and Baltimore, Maryland; the state of Alaska; and the District of Columbia were treated exactly like the 3069 counties in the remainder of the U.S. in aggregating the data into regions.

The basic set of regions is the one defined by the Office of Business Economics and designated 'the OBE Economic Areas of the United States.' This set divides the United States into 173 regions defined on the basis of the economic characteristics of counties but ignoring state boundaries. Most of these regions include at least one Standard Metropolitan Statistical Area. Because comparisons with other studies using only SMSA's, comparisons among SMSA's, contrasts between SMSA and non-SMSA areas, and analysis of non-SMSA areas alone were desired, 193 SMSA's were treated as separate regions in this study. In addition, 12 State Economic Areas, which are composed of whole counties, were substituted for 23 SMSA's in the Northeast which are composed of parts of counties.[1] These SEA's are treated as SMSA's in the study. The result is that the U.S. is partitioned into 377 mutually exclusive, collectively exhaustive regions composed of whole counties: 12 SEA's, 193 SMSA's, and 172 OBE areas outside of SMSA's. (Because one OBE region, San Diego County, California, is also an SMSA, there are only 172 regions which are the non-SMSA parts of OBE regions.) The regions vary in number of counties from 1 to 51.

A general problem of using regions of any feasible size in the type of location analysis pursued here should be noted. The analysis essentially treats each region as a point and data on the location of industries is recorded for those points. When the real spatial extent of a region is considered, however, it must be recognized that industries may be located quite close to each other within a region or may be separated by a considerable distance depending upon the actual size of the region. Furthermore, it is highly likely that regional boundaries separate establishments which actually are geographically associated because the regional boundaries are politically determined county lines. In such a case an agglomerative economy would spill over the regional boundary in the way described in Chapter 1. Note that transport costs could be greater between widely separated establishments in one region than between establishments in adjacent regions, while the assumption of the present study is that they would be larger in the latter case than in the former. In the present study the significance of such problems has not been investigated; it is hoped that their effects in the aggregate for each pair of industries are insignificant.[2]

LOCATION DATA

As indicated in Chapter 1, an objective of the study is to measure the determinants of the locations of firms in manufacturing industries. The problem of choosing an appropriate measure of location of each individual industry therefore confronts the analyst. Ideally, the volume of output in units, or value added, for each industry in each region would be used as a measure of the presence of an industry in each region. Estimated employment for each industry in each region is the measure used in this study. The following paragraphs justify this choice, explain the method of calculation and provide some evaluation of the measure.

The magnitude that would have been most helpful in discovering relationships among different industries, output by region for each industry, is not available because of Census of Manufactures disclosure rules. Some analysts believe that 'technological changes and increasing economies of scale make employment a poor surrogate for output . . .' [46: 8]. The availability of data on this magnitude and the lack of data for any other magnitude as highly correlated with output led to the decision that employment would be used as a proxy for output. Even actual employment figures for all regions and for four-digit industries are not available, however. Census of Population data on industrial employment are not as restricted by disclosure rules as are the Census of Manufactures data but are available only for highly aggregated industries and also are recorded for individuals at place of residence rather than at place of work. Therefore the magnitude used is estimated employment by industry for each region, which is the same magnitude that Richter used in his study.

The data actually available consist of numbers of establishments in seven employment class sizes for each industry by county [51]. Other studies have shown that number of establishments and number of establishments with employment of various class sizes are highly correlated with the number of employees.[3] Median numbers of employees employed by firms in each employment size class are also available, but unfortunately the only median figures are for all industries for the whole U.S.[4] Despite the obvious defects of such aggregate figures, these medians were multiplied by the number of establishments in the seven employment class sizes for each of the 199 industries and 3107 counties and the results aggregated to produce 75,023 X_{ij}'s, estimated employment in industry i in region j, for all $i = 1, 2, \ldots, 199$ industries and $j = 1, 2, \ldots, 377$ regions. The notation for the location data follows:

		Regions			Total estimated industry employment
		1	$\cdots j$	$\cdots 377$	
	1	$X_{1,1}$	$\cdots X_{1,j}$	$\cdots X_{1,377}$	$\sum_j X_{1,j}$
Industries	i	$X_{i,1}$	$\cdots X_{i,j}$	$\cdots X_{i,377}$	$\sum_j X_{i,j}$
	199	$X_{199,1}$	$\cdots X_{199,j}$	$\cdots X_{199,377}$	$\sum_j X_{199,j}$
Total estimated regional employment		$\sum_i X_{i,1}$	$\sum_i X_{i,j}$	$\sum_i X_{i,377}$	

Several types of errors can be made in constructing the estimated employment figures using the available medians for employment in a class size. First it should be recognized that a median cannot be used to reconstruct a total in the same way as can a mean (the median and the number of observations are not sufficient to calculate a total while the mean and the number of observations are). Also the median figures vary from industry to industry in the different class sizes depending upon a wide range of factors including indivisibilities in efficient plant increments. The median may also vary for some industries, or for all industries, from one geographic region to another because of factors such as age of establishments and the technology utilized.

Estimated total U.S. employment for each industry, found by summing the regional estimates, was compared with reported values [52]. It was found that the estimated and reported figures are highly correlated ($R = .96$). Because the distributions of estimated and recorded employment are not known, this statistic is not as valuable as it might be and cannot be tested. If these distributions were normal or approximately normal (which they have been shown not to be by a Kolomogorov-Smirnov test) the correlation would be significant at the .001 level of significance. (Without approximately normal distributions, Fisher's z-transformation does not permit a test.)

Of the estimated figures, 63.8% are within 10% of the reported values (see Table 2–1). Only 17 deviations exceed 10,000 employees. Three of the largest deviations in percentage terms (and two of the three largest in absolute size) are in closely related industries (aircraft, aircraft engines and parts and aircraft propellers and parts). The sum of the absolute deviations for these three industries exceeds the sum of the absolute deviations

Table 2–1. *Comparison of estimated and reported employment totals for included industries.*

Estimated-reported estimated	f	f/Total f	Cumulative percentage
.401 +	5	.025	1.000
.301 + 0.400	6	.031	.975
.201 + 0.300	13	.065	.944
.101 + 0.200	48	.241	.879
.001 + 0.100	127	.638	.638
	199	1.000	

		Reported	Estimated
N	=	199.0000	199.0000
MEAN	=	40232.7035	38910.4925
SDEV	=	65132.4874	54190.0879
MIN	=	1952.0000	1687.0000
MAX	=	649930.0000	533570.0000

for the next 20 industries ranked by percentage deviation. These figures indicate that the use of estimated employment figures in most industries should lead to small errors. Any conclusions regarding those industries for which the deviation of estimated and reported employment is large are, of course, suspect. It is possible, and often desirable, to make use of known totals to adjust the entries within a row or column of a matrix so that the entries sum to the known totals. One adjustment scheme calls for proportionate adjustment of all entries on the assumption that the error of estimation is a bias that is distributed in proportion to the size of each entry. This procedure should be followed when the totals are known and if the individual entries are to be used for further analysis. In the present case, however, the individual entries in the matrix themselves are not used. The row entries, which represent the estimated regional distribution of employment in each industry, are used only to calculate coefficients of correlation. Consequently whether the adjustment is actually made or not is immaterial because coefficients of correlation are unaffected by proportional adjustments to the correlated variables.

Employment in four-digit manufacturing industries is reported for some industries in the largest SMSA's [53]. However, disclosure rules have prevented all industries from having reported figures even for these SMSA's. These data were not used, however, because it was felt that the potential gains from using the reported figures available would be more than offset by loss of consistency. If the estimation procedure outlined above does tend to introduce any systematic bias into estimates for particular industries, substitution of unbiased figures for only some regions is likely to distort any computed spatial relationships for these industries. For example, if the smallest establishments in an industry usually had 19 employees and a few observations of this magnitude were substituted for the median smallest size of six employees, the few regions where the observed values were used would falsely appear to have significantly larger employment in the industry than regions for which only estimates are available.

A random sample of ten industries was chosen from among the 199 used in this study and estimated employment for these industries in the largest SMSA's was compared with recorded employment when such figures were available (see Appendix Table A–6). A total of 52 pairs of estimated and reported figures were identified and found to be highly correlated ($R = .97$). Again this statistic could not be tested for significance. Table 2–2 shows that 71.1% of the estimates are within 10% of the reported values. Only five deviations exceed 1000 employees. These figures indicate that use of estimated employment figures even at the regional level should lead to small errors. Appendix Section A-3 describes minor errors which remain in the regional data. Data from the 1963 Census of Manufacturers was used in this study because, at the time the calculations were performed,

Table 2–2. Comparison of estimated and reported regional industry employment figures.

Estimated-reported estimated	f	f/Total f	Cumulative percentage
.401 +	3	.058	1.000
.301 – .400	2	.039	.942
.201 – .300	3	.058	.903
.101 – .200	7	.134	.845
.051 – .100	14	.269	.711
.000 – .050	23	.442	.442
	52	1.000	

		Reported	Estimated
N	=	52.0000	52.0000
MEAN	=	1934.0962	1948.3269
SDEV	=	2325.9382	2351.7872
MIN	=	121.0000	133.0000
MAX	=	12767.0000	12610.0000

it was the most recent year for which industrial linkage data, described in the following section, was also available.

Additional location data consist of the land area of each region, A_j, and the population of each region, P_j, $j = 1, \ldots, 377$, which are calculated from county figures from the 1960 Census of Population [50]. It is believed that the regional differences in percentage change in population from 1960 to 1963, the date of the regional industry employment data, are small enough to be ignored. (Estimated population figures for 1963 are available for only the larger SMSA's.) These regional population figures are used in the determination of market orientation.

INDUSTRIAL LINKAGE DATA

The data described above provide a basis for measuring the location of industries. In this section the data used to measure the agglomerative economies discussed in Chapter 1 are described. As indicated there, agglomerative economies are derived from reductions in transport cost on inputs and outputs traded by manufacturing firms with other manufacturing firms. To identify potential economies, data on flows of goods are required. Ideally, flows in physical units would be used, but are not available. Instead values of flows are used. When such flows are significantly large, in the sense made clear in Chapter 3, they are called industrial linkages or links.

Data used in this study of identify industrial linkages are derived from the 1963 Input-Output Study [56]. The study divided all U.S. industry into 363 sectors, many of which are four-digit Standard Industrial Classification

Code (SIC) industries. The following paragraphs explain why limiting the study to 199 of the 260 manufacturing industries included in the Input-Output Study was necessary and why the limitation is not a significant detriment to the results of the study.

First, it was felt that the use of some of these industries for meaningful interindustry analysis would be inappropriate because they are composed of more than one four-digit industry. The industries defined by the SIC system are assumed to be truly meaningful. Thus one can argue that any aggregation of these will yield industries that are not strictly comparable to "pure" four-digit SIC industries and that such "nonpure" industries should be omitted. Even at the four-digit SIC industry level of disaggregation problems of heterogeneity arise, but these are significantly less troublesome than at the two and three-digit levels. A basic problem pertaining to the "purity" of industries which remains is the existence of multiproduct establishments. In the regional data compiled by the Bureau of the Census, establishments are classified into a single industry regardless of the number of products produced. Hopefully this problem is minimized to the extent that the multiple products are often products of the same four-digit industry and to the extent that all establishments classified in a single four-digit industry have similar multiple product outputs. The existence of multi-product establishments is just one possible complication which cannot be handled adequately, regardless of the particular scheme used for assigning establishments to industries.[5] Artle has pointed out that "It is by no means certain that the remedy [for nonhomogeneous industries] is to have more sectors" [2: 11]. He points out that at every level of aggregation above the single establishment, problems of nonhomogeneity will exist.

An additional factor which led to the selection of 199 of the 260 manufacturing industries in the 1963 Input-Output Study was the need to limit the size of the location matrix to one that could be handled without extraordinary programming efforts by the IBM 360/75 computer at the University of Illinois. This meant essentially limiting the total number of elements in the geographic matrix to significantly less than 80×10^3. Because the number of regions to be used was close to 400, the number of industries had to be limited to approximately 200, and this round number was chosen early in the analysis for preliminary calculations and reduced only when it was found that geographic data were not available for one industry originally selected. (See Appendix A, Section A–2, for a description of the selection of the particular industries used and Appendix Table A–4 for a list of the 199 industries.)

There are difficulties in limiting the study in either number of regions or number of industries. It was felt that the retention of the complete geographic scope was preferable for several reasons. First, as indicated above, the manufacturing industries were limited at the outset because the available input-output data was not for single four-digit industries. No comparable barrier to using the complete set of regions existed, however. Second, as also indicated above, the treatment of non-manufacturing industries places certain limitations on the study initially. Agglomeration economies in this study are possible when spatial juxtaposition of firms in different manufacturing industries will permit reductions in transportation costs on traded inputs and outputs. Potential reductions in transportation costs on output sold to final demand are viewed as encouraging market orientation and potential reductions in transportation costs on inputs purchased from all primary resource suppliers as a whole are viewed as encouraging resource orientation. Inputs and outputs traded with the service, government and foreign sectors are ignored. Thus the study does not even intend to treat all U.S. industry equivalently or to include all in the same manner. The exclusion of some manufacturing industries is simply an extension of this uneven treatment of industries.

A third reason for limiting the industrial rather than the geographic scope of the study is that the type of industrial interrelationships used are not dependent upon the inclusion of all industries. The errors that may occur because of restricting the number of industries are either in 1. not identifying *all* industries which show locational effects of agglomerative economies toward each other or 2. a probability that significant geographic associations are not included. Those relationships identified as being significant locational factors will not be affected by the exclusion of some industries; only their relative importance might be affected.

A consequence of limiting the scope of the study to only 199 manufacturing industries is that in so doing the estimated regional employment totals

			Input industries				
		1	... j	...	199	Final demand	Total industry output
Output industries	1	$Y_{1,1}$	... $Y_{1,j}$	... $Y_{1,199}$		$Y_{1,D}$	$\sum_j Y_{1,j}$
	i	$Y_{i,1}$	... $Y_{i,j}$	... $Y_{i,199}$		$Y_{i,D}$	$\sum_j Y_{i,j}$
	199	$Y_{199,1}$	... $Y_{199,j}$	... $Y_{199,199}$		$Y_{199,D}$	$\sum_j Y_{199,j}$
Total inter-mediate inputs		I_1	I_j		I_{199}		

are the sums of estimated employment in only 199 industries. Fortunately these totals are only used in the construction of the general agglomerative economies variable in Chapter 5. The figures there suggest that the underestimates of total regional employment do not seriously affect the results.

The basic input-output data used are 39601 $Y_{i,j}$'s, value of output industry i sells to industry j for all $i, j = 1, 2, \ldots, 199$ industries. They may be expressed as in the table on page 21.[6]

$Y_{i,D}$ is the sales of the output of industry i to final demand as defined in Chapter 3, and I_j is the input purchases of industry j from all manufacturing sectors, also discussed in Chapter 3. Total industry output, $\Sigma_j Y_{i,j}$, for each industry is the sum of its sales to *all* other sectors and not just to the manufacturing industries used in this study.

SUMMARY

This chapter has described the set of regions used in this study to describe the locational patterns of manufacturing firms in the U.S., the data to be used in measuring the location of firms in each manufacturing industry and the data to be used in identifying potential agglomerative economies. The following chapter will show how each of the location factors identified in Chapter 1 is measured.

NOTES

1. The result of using SEA's rather than SMSA's in the Northeast is shown in Section A–1 and Appendix Table A–1, A–2 and A–3.
2. Klaassen [25] has argued that no single set of regions is appropriate for industrial location analysis but that there is a 'relevant' region for each industry which essentially is a combination of the industry's market and supply areas. Such an approach is possible only for the study of the location of individual industries. In the present study the joint locational distributions of pairs of industries are of primary interest and thus a single set of regions for all industries is necessary.
3. See Morrison, *et al.* [37] and Alexander and Lindberg [1] for examples.
4. The seven employment class sizes and their medians (M) are: (1) 1–19, M = 6; (2) 20–49, M = 31; (3) 50–99, M = 69; (4) 100–249, M = 155; (5) 250–499, M = 346; (6) 500–999, M = 684; (7) 1000 or more, M = 2545.
5. In the extreme one could probably find a basis for considering each establishment to be an "industry." Perhaps the most systematic method of deciding how much disaggregation is useful would be to compute measures of "information" in the way that accountants do to determine the appropriate level of disaggregation for an income statement or balance sheet.
6. It should be noted that in the 1963 Input-Output Study flows of goods valued at less than $500.00 are recorded as zeroes.

3. Measurement of factors influencing industrial location

This chapter examines how the location factor orientations described in Chapter 1 can be measured. First, however, a measure of randomness in location is developed. The proposition that a significant proportion of manufacturing firms in the U.S. has located systematically, and therefore is not 'footloose,' is tested using this measure of randomness. Measures of the various factor orientations of industries are then developed for use in explaining geographic location in Chapter 5. Potential labor orientation is measured using the ratio of wages to value added. Market orientation is measured using the proportion of outputs sold to final demand sectors and the degree of geographic association of firms in an industry with final demand markets. Material orientation is measured using the proportion of inputs obtained from primary resource extractors and the degree of geographic association of firms in an industry with resource areas. Potential agglomerative economies are identified using flows of inputs and outputs between pairs of manufacturing industries. Potential agglomerative economies affecting more than two industries are examined in Chapter 4.

NONRANDOMNESS IN LOCATION

Some investigations have concluded that a very large proportion of industry in the U.S. is footloose or free to locate in any of a large number of locations based upon primarily noneconomic factors [40: 80]. If this is true, one might expect a greater degree of dispersion or randomness in location than if nonrandomly distributed economic factors are important in determining the locations of most firms. While randomness in location is not a perfect substitute for the degree to which industries are footloose, an investigation of randomness may nevertheless yield significant information in this regard. The following analysis of nonrandomness in location is similar to that of Artle except that, while Artle's analysis was concerned with locations of retail establishments in homogeneous land areas of a single metropolitan area, the following is concerned neither with the location of specific individual firms nor with land areas [2: 133–135].

The procedures described in the following paragraphs are not the only ones that might be used. Here, and elsewhere in this study, the author has attempted to select reasonable and justifiable procedures while recognizing that a variety of other procedures might be reasonable for other purposes or to other investigators.

The approach followed below defines randomness in location to mean that firms locate their plants among the 377 regions described in Chapter 2 randomly. A test for nonrandomness then consists of comparing the actual distribution of plants with a distribution that would be expected if the pattern was random by means of a chi-square test. Several adjustments to this procedure as well as two possible interpretations of the random comparison distribution are described below.

The first problem confronted is that existing plants may not be the best measure of a firm's location decisions. A very large plant may result from the decision to place a number of more basic units of productive capacity at a given location, possibly to take advantage of any economies of scale that might exist within the firm. Thus the large plant in a single region should receive more weight than a small plant in another region when comparing with a hypothetical random distribution. Essentially one is interested in the spatial distribution of capacity in an industry and not simply the number of plants.

If this is accepted, one is then confronted with the necessity of defining the basic unit for each industry. One might assume that the smallest level of operation observed in an industry among all geographic regions in which that industry is present at a non-zero level, minimum $X_{ij} = MIN_i$, is the level at which a firm in that industry can operate economically in any single location. This level might be of sufficient magnitude to permit the firm to reap the benefits of a large part of any economies of scale within the firm and/or industry which are possible for firms in the industry.[1]

If the total output of any industry, $\Sigma_j X_{ij}$, is divided by this smallest size, MIN_i, which might be thought of as the minimum 'efficient' level of output, the result is a number that can be interpreted as the maximum number of geographically separate, economically feasible operations of which that industry is capable.[2] The integer value of this number can be used as a proxy for the number of basic units or firm clusters, n_i, in the industry, i, which must be located in the j regions.

Now one must specify what a 'random' distribution of the n_i clusters would be. It might be quite realistic to assume that firms locating their clusters 'randomly' would choose the various regions with other than equal probability. Randomness could mean that the probability of a given firm locating in a given region was equal to the proportion of: a. total population in that region, b. industrial activity (dollar value or employment) in that region, or c. total land area in that region. However, proportions of total population and industrial activity are undesirable measures because these magnitudes reflect the presence of a given set of industries to the extent that people locate near jobs more than the converse. Proportion of land area is undesirable because not only land area, but also the characteristics of the land, are important locational considerations. It is both difficult and hazardous to subject the qualitative characteristics of land to a precise quantitative analysis.[3] For the above reasons it is assumed here that randomness means random selection among regions with equal probability of choosing each region. One difficulty which does remain unresolved is that the regions used in this study are defined on the basis of the locational decisions which firms have made in the past. (The regions are delineated on the basis of economic activities at locations.)

Each of the n_i clusters in each of the $i = 1, \ldots, 199$ industries must locate in one of the 377 regions. If clusters decide among the alternative regions with equal probability (randomly), then the probability of choosing any specific region is $p = 1/377$. In considering any single region, each cluster may be located there or not, and thus the probability that C_{ij} of the n_i clusters in industry i are located in a specific region, j, can be found as the binomial probability,

$$B_i(c_{ij} = C_{ij} | n_i, p) = \frac{n_i!}{C_{ij}!(n_i - C_{ij})!} p^{C_{ij}} (1 - p)^{n_i - C_{ij}},$$

or because p is small, as the Poisson probability,

$$P_i(c_{ij} = C_{ij} | n_i, p) = \frac{(n_i p) e^{C_{ij} - n_i p}}{C_{ij}!}$$

The expected number of regions in which each possible number of clusters ($c_{ij} = 0, 1, \ldots, n_i$) appears is found as $P_i \times 377$. The distribution of observed numbers of regions with each possible number of clusters is then compared with the distribution of expected numbers by means of an appropriate statistical test such as the chi-square. The format for such a test is indicated below:

C_{ij} Number of clusters in a region	$P_i(c_{ij} = C_{ij})$ Binomial or poisson probability of number	$E_{ij} = (377)P_i(c_{ij} = C_{ij})$ Expected number of regions	0_{ij} Observed number of regions
0	$P_i(c_{ij} = 0)$	$E_{i,0}$	$0_{i,0}$
1	$P_i(c_{ij} = 1)$	$E_{i,1}$	$0_{i,1}$
.	.	.	.
.	.	.	.
.	.	.	.
n_i	$P_i(c_{ij} = n_i)$	$E_{i,ni}$	$0_{i,ni}$

$x_i^2 = \sum_j \dfrac{(0_{ij} - E_{ij})^2}{E_{ij}}$. If $x_i^2 > x_{i,\alpha}^2$ reject the hypothesis that clusters in industry are randomly located.

Because of the large numbers involved (n_i ranges from 280 to approximately 100,000) and the cost of performing such a test many times, an alternative to the above test is used. The expected number of clusters of industry i located in each region is assumed to be $(n_i)p$, where $p = 1/377$. The rectangular distribution of expected numbers of clusters is compared to the observed number in each region by means of a X^2 test similar to the one above utilizing data which can be presented as follows:

Region number	$E_{i,j}$ Expected number of clusters	$0_{i,j}$ Observed number of clusters
1	$E_{i,1} = n_i p$	$0_{i,1}$
2	$E_{i,2} = n_i p$	$0_{i,2}$
.	.	.
.	.	.
.	.	.
377	$E_{i,377} = n_i p$	$0_{i,377}$

The X^2 statistic is then calculated as above. More formally then, industry is NOT RANDOMLY LOCATED if, and only if:

$$X_i^2 \geq X_{i,\alpha}^2$$

where: α is a preselected level of statistical significance (.95 in this case); $X_{i,\alpha}^2$ is the value of X^2 which, if exceeded, permits one to conclude that the observed distribution is different from the one that would be expected if industrial location of plants was random over all locations; and where

$$X_i^2 = \sum_j \frac{(0_{ij} - n_i/377)}{n_i/377}, \quad n_i = \sum_j X_{ij}/MIN_i$$

$$0_{ij} = X_{ij}/MIN_i$$

$$MIN_i = \text{Minimum } (X_{ij})_j$$

If clusters of firms in the various industries are not 'randomly' located, one would expect that for significantly more industries than not, the results of the above test would indicate that the distributions are different. All of the 199 industries used in this study were found to be non-randomly located by the above measure. Examination of the individual industry distributions reveals the reason for this result. For most industries, there are a large number of regions in which the observed number of clusters is zero. In such cases, the value of X^2 is increased by the value of the expected number of clusters for each zero observation region and, since the smallest level of presence is six for all but five industries, this expected number of clusters is a large number. While this result is not very helpful and a better method of testing for randomness should be devised, the results show, at least, that there is not a strong degree of randomness in the location of manufacturing industries.

As mentioned in the preceding paragraphs, the minimum estimated regional employment figure is found to be six (the median of the 1 to 19 employees size class) in 194 of the 199 industries.[4] This might be interpreted as evidence contrary to the existence of economies of scale on a widespread basis except for several other possibilities. First, it is undoubtedly true that, even at the four-digit SIC level of aggregation, many industries are not homogeneous. For example, an industry such as aircraft engines and parts might include some very small firms supplying a specialized part to one or more of the large aircraft engine manufacturers, thus establishing an uncharacteristically low minimum size for the industry. Second, the boundary problem described earlier may affect the minimum reported size. If a single small firm is part of a larger cluster of firms which have located in proximity to each other in order to reduce costs, but the single firm happens to be located outside the region where the remainder of the cluster is located, then an uncharacteristically low minimum would again be established. Third, isolated small establishments may exist profitably in industries with relatively high transportation costs and small economies of scale. This possibility could be checked by examining the location and cost structures of specific small establishments.

Alternatives to using the minimum size of six for most industries were considered but rejected. The number of establishments in each industry might have been used to calculate an average size of establishment, but use of this average would fail to deal with the existence of isolated small establishments. Examination of the distributions of employment by region for each industry might have revealed that in a number of industries very small establishments were atypical and that a somewhat larger minimum size, possibly excluding the lower tail of each distribution, might have been chosen, but the computational requirements would have exceeded the scope of the present study.

THE ORIENTATION OF INDUSTRIES

Having determined that firms in the 199 industries of this study are nonrandomly located by the above test (and thus may not be footloose), the effects of the location factors identified in Chapter 1 can be examined. In the remainder of this chapter measures of the factor orientations are developed. Methods used in identifying industries as potentially labor oriented, marked oriented or material oriented are presented first because these are more readily understood than agglomerative economy orientation. The results of applying these methods to the 199 manufacturing industries selected for this study are also presented. The method of identifying potential agglomerative economies is then discussed.

Labor orientation

A firm is said to be labor oriented if it chooses its location in such a way as to take advantage of labor conditions in a particular region. Labor orientation differs from other orientations, as explained in Chapter 1, to the extent that labor costs either attract a firm to the region to take advantage of the lower labor costs or they have no effect at all, while the other factors have effects which may produce intermediate locations. Labor orientation of firms may be the result of a number of different factors. Greenhut separates these into conditions regarding 1. wage levels, 2. productivity, 3. turnover and work stoppage rates, 4. supply of laborers and 5. labor laws which may vary from location to location and industry to industry [15: 129–135]. All of these affect production costs directly or indirectly. Lichtenberg differentiates labor orientation in low-skill industries from that in high-skill industries [29: 48–56]. In this study only direct production labor costs will be used to identify potentially labor oriented industries. All authors seem to agree with Fuchs that 'labor costs will exert a locational pull in proportion to the part that labor costs play in total costs' [14: 165]. A particular measure of labor orientation advocated by Fuchs, Greenhut and Klaassen [25b] is the ratio of wages to value added.[5]

The ratio of value added to wages, V_i/W_i (which is simply the inverse of wages to value added), is the measure used to identify potential labor orientation in the present study.[6] Table 3–1 lists the ratio in column 6 for each industry in column 1. Careful inspection of the ratios for all industries indicates that a value of 2.65 places most industries commonly thought of as being potentially labor oriented, such as the textile and footwear industries, into that category.[7] (Potentially labor oriented industries are indicated by an asterisk next to the entry in column 6 of Table 3–1.) Fuchs refers to industries with ratios of wages to value added lower than the *mean* as labor intensive [14: 167]. This is probably because he did not examine the distribution of ratios. Of the 199 industries used in the present study, 139 have values of V_i/W_i below the mean. It should be noted that the value of 2.65 has meaning only for 1963 data because the ratio is changing over time in all industries (rising in most).

Certainly one would be more satisfied if a critical value could be selected more scientifically. The problem is that we are not attempting to decide

Table 3–1. Summary of market, material and labor orientations by industry.

Industry number (1)	Orientation[a] (2)	Proportion of output sold to final demand (3)	Correlation between employment & population (4)	Proportion of inputs bought from resource extractors (5)	Ratio of value added to wages (6)
1	1		.915	.000	2.492*
2	3	.571*	.015	.570*	3.590
3	3	.593*	.101	.370*	2.907
4	3	.335*	.105	.315*	4.686
5	2	.896*	.912	.178*	5.656
6	2	.700*	.872	.587*	6.141
7	2,3	.796*	.419	.412*	3.319
8	2,3	.769*	.324	.105*	5.857
9	3	.400*	.097	.333*	3.706
10	2	.717*	.603	.077*	4.278
11	2,3	.890*	.192	.524*	2.655
12	3	.114*	.404	.186*	6.184
13	3	.289*	.033	.702*	6.337
14	3	.022	.168	.450*	4.455
15	2	.262*	.809	.051	15.930
16	3		.010	.599*	3.875
17	3		.107	.826*	5.917
18	3		.292	.304*	5.275
19	0		.836	.030	3.772
20	2	.807*	.522	.000	11.118
21	2	.475*	.387	.026	4.830
22	2	.816*	.856	.001	4.534
23	2	.798*	.795	.146*	5.855
24	3		.021	.609*	2.388*
25	1	.042	.227	.000	2.364*
26	3	.109*	.071	.112*	2.622*
27	1	.225*	.356	.001	1.976*
28	1		.549	.018	2.607*
29	1		.243	.000	2.406*
30	0		.405	.001	3.063
31	1		.028	.047	2.406*
32	3		.186	.433*	2.292*
33	1	.034	.430	.056	2.167*
34	0	.075*	.515	.005	3.435
35	2	.724*	.782	.000	2.339*
36	2	.784*	.804	.000	2.783
37	3	.025	−.015	.676*	2.048*
38	1		.004	.000	1.961*
39	1		.104	.000	1.897*
40	1		.021	.000	1.846*
41	1		.650	.000	2.177*
42	1		.017	.000	1.988*
43	0		.223	.000	3.121
44	0		.146	.002	2.685
45	2	.171*	.692	.001	2.280*
46	2	.794*	.443	.000	2.246*
47	2	.657*	.769	.000	2.685

Table 3–1 continued

Industry number (1)	Orientation[a] (2)	Proportion of output sold to final demand (3)	Correlation between employment & population (4)	Proportion of inputs bought from resource extractors (5)	Ratio of value added to wages (6)
48	2	.808*	.651	.000	3.018
49	1		.266	.001	2.409*
50	1		.901	.000	2.053*
51	0		.676	.000	2.715
52	2	.663*	.434	.000	2.904
53	1		.783	.001	2.286*
54	0		.005	.008	3.651
55	0	.006	.069	.024	2.723
56	0		.216	.025	3.628
57	1	.018	.804	.000	2.405*
58	2	.723*	.250	.000	4.243
59	2	.246*	.778	.000	20.573
60	2	.165*	.834	.000	5.183
61	0	.003	.342	.004	4.546
62	0		.058	.023	3.354
63	0		−.008	.008	5.568
64	2	.780*	.742	.000	13.332
65	0	.009	.764	.003	6.057
66	0	.006	.400	.001	7.222
67	0		.728	.177	4.138
68	0	.370*	.229	.008	2.872
69	2	.930*	.194	.000	2.051*
70	0	.041	.839	.000	2.864
71	1	.002	.280	.000	2.217*
72	1	.004	.235	.054	2.259*
73	3		.075	.315*	4.518
74	3		.206	.228*	2.111*
75	1		.361	.041	2.525*
76	1		.068	.025	2.382*
77	3		.131	.098*	2.226*
78	1		.098	.043	2.189*
79	1	.378*	.468	.018	2.234*
80	0		.783	.169*	3.375
81	0	.002	.764	.170*	2.828
82	3		.114	.347*	3.336
83	3	.243*	.218	.269*	1.972*
84	0	.059	.380	.018	3.869
85	1	.002	.491	.040	2.580*
86	3		.497	.383*	3.444
87	0		.220	.002	2.994
88	3		.265	.128	3.339
89	0	.077*	.637	.013	2.923
90	3		.133	.296*	3.663
91	3		.056	.122*	2.230
92	3		.070	.442*	2.726
93	3		.049	.076*	4.203
94	0		.808	.000	3.771

Table 3-1 continued

Industry number (1)	Orientation[a] (2)	Proportion of output sold to final demand (3)	Correlation between employment & population (4)	Proportion of inputs bought from resource extractors (5)	Ratio of value added to wages (6)
95	1		.197	.001	2.390*
96	0		.193	.000	3.384
97	0	.001	.595	.000	2.812
98	1	.012	.427	.006	1.974*
99	1		.605	.006	2.214*
100	1		.729	.006	2.148*
101	1		.372	.002	1.994*
102	1		.143	.000	2.199*
103	0		.669	.001	2.938
104	0		.627	.000	2.670
105	2	.760*	.271	.001	4.875
106	0	.039	.457	.001	2.775
107	0		.415	.000	2.656
108	0	.063	.491	.001	3.209
109	1		.670	.000	2.326*
110	0		.812	.000	2.767
111	1		.522	.000	2.480*
112	1		.898	.000	2.394*
113	0	.016	.723	.000	3.260
114	1	.080*	.723	.000	2.413*
115	1	.019	.791	.000	2.527*
116	1		.495	.000	2.435*
117	1		.395	.000	2.207*
118	1		.157		2.069*
119	0	.112*	.421		2.916
120	0	.058	.846	.003	2.849
121	0		.191	.003	2.680
122	0	.074	.180	.001	2.822
123	0	.003	.134	.001	2.786
124	0		.365	.001	2.814
125	0		.134	.001	3.183
126	0		.457	.000	4.060
127	0		.340	.000	3.616
128	1	.012	.224	.001	2.569*
129	1		.459	.000	2.620*
130	0		.525	.000	3.223
131	1		.140	.001	2.434*
132	1	.068	.418	.001	3.204
133	1		.325	.000	2.642*
134	0		.757	.000	2.737
135	0		.595	.000	2.833
136	1		.299	.001	2.386*
137	0		.444	.000	3.129
138	0		.389	.001	2.725
139	0		.206	.000	3.856
140	0		.531	.000	2.981
141	0	.210*	.018	.001	3.422

Table 3–1 continued

Industry number (1)	Orientation[a] (2)	Proportion of output sold to final demand (3)	Correlation between employment & population (4)	Proportion of inputs bought from resource extractors (5)	Ratio of value added to wages (6)
142	0	.111*	.233	.001	3.231
143	0		.437	.001	3.551
144	0		.295	.001	3.016
145	0	.127*	.449	.000	3.327
146	0		.267	.000	3.961
147	0	.068	.624	.000	3.752
148	0		.618	.000	3.377
149	0	.005	.595	.000	3.161
150	1	.006	.336	.001	2.622*
151	0		.179	.000	3.592
152	0		.369	.000	3.640
153	0		.192	.004	3.209
154	0	.001	.434	.000	2.971
155	2	.756*	.415	.001	3.047
156	0	.586*	.134	.001	2.974
157	0	.742*	.059	.001	4.121
158	2	.551*	.476	.000	3.655
159	0	.715*	.044	.000	5.123
160	0	.155*	.336	.000	2.709
161	0	.289*	.479	.000	3.761
162	0	.397*	.218	.017	3.641
163	2	.141*	.870	.000	3.038
164	2	.665*	.530	.000	3.152
165	2	.834*	.381	.000	3.802
166	0		.453	.001	2.826
167	0	.007	.792	.000	3.517
168	0		.400	.000	2.772
169	1	.020	.769	.000	2.646*
170	0	.290*	.422	.000	3.043
171	0	.386*	.106	.003	3.920
172	0		.287	.000	4.300
173	0	.065	.400	.001	2.693
174	0	.220*	.479	.000	3.035
175	1		.217	.000	2.333*
176	1		.272	.000	2.515*
177	2	.393*	.421	.001	3.174
178	0	.007	.560	.000	3.485
179	0		.371	.000	3.180
180	0	.001	.070		3.012
181	1		.609	.000	2.638*
182	1		.436	.000	1.655*
183	0		.249	.002	2.763
184	1		.324	.001	2.366*
185	2	.815*	.198	.000	2.471*
186	1	.201*	.454	.001	2.477*
187	0		.656	.000	2.992
188	0	.112*	.595	.000	3.287
189	0	.043	.422	.000	2.798

Table 3–1 continued

Industry number (1)	Orientation[a] (2)	Proportion of output sold to final demand (3)	Correlation between employment & population (4)	Proportion of inputs bought from resource extractors (5)	Ratio of value added to wages (6)
190	0	.024	.565	.000	3.209
191	0	.199*	.581	.011	4.316
192	0		.749	.002	3.532
193	0	.190*	.558	.004	5.049
194	2	.442*	.562	.001	2.341*
195	2	.861*	.731	.000	3.058
196	2	.501*	.547	.000	2.928
197	2	.343*	.711	.000	2.410*
198	2	.306*	.547	.075*	3.391
199	0	.623*	.079	.019	4.030
Mean		.166	.410	.006	3.416
Stand. dev.		.273	.255	.152	2.025
Criterion for Indication		>.075		>.075	<2.650
Indicator		*		*	*
Number indicated		68		35	66

a. 0, 1, 2 and 3 refer respectively to no identified orientation, potential labor orientation, market orientation, and material orientation.

whether or not a given measured value for the ratio V_i/W_i is of a size such that we can conclude that it came from a distribution with a hypothesized parameter. A priori one has no grounds for expecting that any point in the distribution of values would be sufficient to identify potential labor orientation. The values must be calibrated by using the values for industries whose behavior is understood a priori. Klaassen simply suggested that the lower the value, the more labor oriented a firm might be and labeled values less than 2.17 as 'moderately high' [25b: 37].

It is recognized that firms in certain industries with relatively low ratios may nevertheless locate primarily in response to other factors, especially if labor costs in those industries are essentially constant over most geographic regions. It would be possible to examine wage data from different regions to determine whether labor costs actually do vary significantly from region to region in each industry, but this would exceed the scope of the present study. Based on the data in Table 3–1, 65 industries are preliminarily identified as potentially labor oriented. This number is reduced to 51 by eliminating, for reasons discussed in the following sections, those identified as market or material oriented. These 51 industries are indicated by a 1 in column 2 of Table 3–1. Formally industry is POTENTIALLY

LABOR ORIENTED if, and only if:

(1) $X_i^2 > X_{i,\alpha}^2$
(2) $L_i < 2.65$
(3) Industry i is not MARKET ORIENTED
(4) Industry i is not MATERIAL ORIENTED

where $L_i = V_i / W_i$.

Market orientation
Market orientation is one of the traditional explanations for industrial location. Market orientation results from a firm's attempt to reduce the cost of transporting the output that it sells to final consumers by locating near the market where these sales are made. In order to identify market orientation, two things are needed: 1. a measure of the potential attraction of the market and 2. a measure of the response of firms in the industry to the market.

In this study an industry's sales to final demand are used as the measure of the potential attractiveness of the market.[8] A means of specifying the location of the market is needed before a firm's response to that market can be estimated. Despite Harris' finding that while 'population is one measure of the market, ... retail sales appear to provide the most valuable single index of the total final market for commercial goods,' [16: 319] population is used as a measure of the market in the present study because of the difficulty of obtain regional retail sales estimates.[9] The correlation coefficient computed between industry level in a region (X_{ij}) and population of the region (P_j) over all regions $(j = 1, \ldots, 377)$, $R_{x_i \cdot p}$, provides a measure of the response of firms in the industry to the market.

Spiegelman is among those for whom 'an association between the distribution of an industry and the total population or income indicates the orientation of that industry to consumer markets' [44: 23].[10] In this study, however, market orientation is identified only for those industries for which the coefficient of correlation between industry level and population, $R_{x_i \cdot p}$, is high, and the proportion of output sold to final demand, F_i, is also high. The second criterion eliminates from the group of market oriented industries those that are strongly linked to market oriented industries but do not sell significant proportions of their own total output to final demand. The second criterion also reduces the probability of identifying as market oriented those industries that are actually oriented toward large labor markets which coincide with population centers.[11]

Table 3–1 identifies, with a 2 in column 2, 36 industries which are considered to be market oriented in this study. For these industries 1. the

product of the proportion of output sold to final demand sectors, F_i, and the correlation coefficient between population and employment, $R_{x_i \cdot p}$, is greater than .1, and 2. their sum is greater than .8, or, more formally:
Industry i is MARKET ORIENTED if, and only if:

(1) $X_i^2 > X_{i,\alpha}$
(2) $(R_{x_i \cdot p} \cdot F_i) > .1$
and (3) $(R_{x_i \cdot p} + F_i) > .8$

where $F_i = X_{F,i}/X_{i.}$ and $X_{F,i}$ is the value of output sold to final demand sectors. The critical values, .1 and .8, were determined by carefully examining the distributions of F_i and $X_{F,i}$ and particularly the values for some industries generally accepted as being market oriented (such as bakery products). It was found that separate critical values for each measure independently could not be established to yield expected results for those industries with known locational orientations. Similarly neither their product nor their sum yielded acceptable results alone. The combination of the two does yield expected results. On the assumption that similar values will identify similar orientations among the industries whose orientations are not known in advance, the above criteria can thus be used.

Because the objective of the analysis is not to determine whether or not either value, or any combination of them, is large enough to accept the hypothesis that the observed value came from a distribution with a parameter of hypothesized magnitude, the usual statistical inference methods are not helpful in establishing the critical values. The statistical populations of interest for each industry are not the populations of $R_{x_i \cdot p}$ or F_i for all i but rather the populations of values which might have been observed for each industry and from which a single value has been drawn. The objective instead is to decide when observed behavior, as measured by $R_{x_i \cdot p}$ and F_i indicates that market orientation exists.[12]

Material orientation
Another of the classical orientations of industries was to materials or input sites. Material orientation, as used here, refers to the location of a firm near firms in the primary resource extracting sector of the economy in order to reduce transport costs on primary inputs. Food processing, lumber processing and primary metal industries are typical examples of industries thought to be material oriented. The use of primary resources often results in a net weight loss from primary inputs to final product. The resultant transport cost savings on the processed product provide the classic motivation for a firm to locate near its source of primary resource. Firms using the products of primary resource extractors are called first stage resource users. Another

meaning for material orientation could be derived from a broader interpretation of the term 'material' to include products of first stage resource
users.[13] This interpretation is not adopted for the present study because
the lack of a precise means of defining various stage resource users seems
to make it more meaningful to treat links between manufacturing industries
of all types together.

Richter identified as first stage resource users those industries that pur-
chase more than 7.5% of their inputs from primary resource extractors. The
7.5 figure placed most industries usually considered to be first stage resource users into that category.[14] For comparative purposes, first stage
resource users will be identified in this study also as industries purchasing
more than 7.5% of their inputs from primary resource extractors and will be
referred to as potentially material oriented industries.[15] Column 5 of Table
3–1 lists the percentage of inputs purchased from primary resource extractors. Those purchasing more than 7.5% are indicated by an asterisk. Table
3–2 lists the primary resource extracting industries in the 1963 Input-Output Study.

Just as market orientation of an industry requires two criteria for identification – an indication of the potential economy possible from reducing
transport costs and an indication of locational response to the potential
economy – so too does material orientation. Material orientation thus will
be identified only when the potential material orientation of an industry, as
indicated by a linkage between the industry and the primary extractive

Table 3–2. List of primary resource extracting industries.

1963 Input-Output study number	Title
1.01	Dairy farm products
1.02	Poultry and eggs
1.03	Meat, animals and miscellaneous livestock products
2.01	Cotton
2.02	Food feed grains and grass seeds
2.03	Tobacco
2.04	Fruits and tree nuts
2.05	Vegetables, sugar and miscellaneous crops
2.06	Oil bearing crops
2.07	Forest, greenhouse and nursery products
3.00	Forestry and fishery products
4.00	Agricultural, forestry and fishery services
5.00	Iron and ferroalloy ores mining
6.01	Copper ore mining
6.02	Nonferrous metal ores mining, except copper
7.00	Coal mining
8.00	Crude petroleum and natural gas
9.00	Stone and clay mining and quarrying
10.00	Chemical and fertilizer mineral mining

sector, has been realized in geographic location. For lack of a more sophisticated criterion, evidence of the realization of the potential economy in the present study is a correlation between the distribution of population and the distribution of industry employment, $R_{x_i \cdot p}$, of less than .5.[16] This is based on the rather heroic assumption that primary resource extractors are usually not located in or near population centers. For some industries this assumption may be highly questionable (such as for dairy farm products) but, on the whole, it seems justifiable on intuitive grounds. Table 3–1 identifies, with a 3 in column 2, 28 industries which are considered to be material oriented in the present study. For these industries the proportion of inputs purchased from primary resource extractors, S_i, is greater than .075 and the correlation between industry employment and population, $R_{x_i \cdot p}$, is less than .5, or, more formally:

Industry i is MATERIAL ORIENTED if, and only if:

(1) $X_i^2 > X_{i,\alpha}^2$
(2) $R_{x_i \cdot p} < .5$
and (3) $S_i > .075$

where $S_i = X_{S,i}/X_i$ and $X_{S,i}$ is the value of inputs purchased from primary resource extractors. Again the values are derived from examining the values of $R_{x_i \cdot p}$ and S_i for industries whose locational orientations are known with confidence and assuming that similar values will identify similar orientations.

None of the types of orientation identified in this study are mutually exclusive (even though market orientation requires a high value for the coefficient of correlation with population and material orientation requires a low value for this coefficient). The results reported in column 2 of Table 3–1 show that some industries may be identified as having more than one type of orientation with the procedures employed. Strong statements regarding the orientation of particular industries are possible only when a single orientation is identified. However, it is possible to say that the list of potentially labor oriented industries should omit the 14 industries which are identified as being either market oriented or material oriented because the latter two types of orientation use stronger criteria than potential labor orientation. There are three industries identified by the criteria detailed above as being both market and material oriented. All of these are food processors for whom perishability of a resource that is also used directly by final consumers dictates a resource location which coincides with the market for the resource.

Of the 199 industries listed in Table 3–1, 87 (indicated by 0 in column 2) have none of the three orientations discussed in the preceding sections. These may be industries that a better test for randomness would have identified as being randomly oriented, as discussed further in Chapter 5, or they may be viewed as prime candidates for agglomerative orientation as discussed in the next section and in Chapters 4 and 5.

Agglomerative economy orientation

The preceding sections have described how industries are identified as nonrandom, potentially labor oriented, market oriented or material oriented. This section will describe how potential agglomerative orientation is identified using industrial linkages derived from input-output data. The following chapter will discuss how realized potential agglomerative economies are identified across regions.

Weber's industrial location theory was among the earliest to incorporate the intuitively appealing proposition that, other things being equal, profit-maximizing entrepreneurs who trade their products with one another will attempt to locate their industrial establishment near to each other in order to minimize the necessary costs of transportation on the traded products. As noted earlier this behavior has resulted in industries being identified as market, material or agglomeration oriented. In the present study such locations are identified as agglomeration oriented except in industries that are market or material oriented as discussed in the preceding sections. Potential agglomerative economies based on cost reducing factors other than input and output trading, such as the sharing of services and labor pools or other resources, are not identified here.[17]

Values of flows of inputs and outputs between firms in different industries are the substance of input-output analysis and input-output tables are valuable in the study of industrial location primarily because they conveniently summarize much relevant information that may be interpreted as evidence of potential economies of spatial juxtaposition which may be agglomerative forces. Potential agglomerative economies are identified in the present study, using input-output data, even though such data have limitations as described below, because better data are not available. In addition, and in spite of the ciriticism offered below, the dollar magnitudes of the flows of products between two industries are used as indicators of the magnitudes of potential locational economies.[18]

Hoover and Streit have correctly criticized the use of input-output tables to measure locational attraction as a practice that, in the words of Hoover, 'assumes that the money value of A's sales to B are a good measure of the locational attraction between the two industries' [19: 11].[19] A problem arises because it is entirely possible for some firms to have their ultimate locations absolutely 'determined' by the existence of a relatively small-valued flow of product. An example might be a firm producing a product requiring an extremely heavy, but cheap, input, the weight of which is not substantially added to the final product (a weight-losing product). On the other hand, very large value flows may be of no locational consequence if transportation costs for high-valued inputs are insignificant.

Hoover has suggested construction of a different kind of input-output table for use in locational analysis [19: 12]. He would tabulate the costs per unit of distance of transferring the inputs that industry B purchases from industry A 1. per unit of industry B's output and 2. per unit of industry A's output. The first of these would measure the transfer cost incentive for industry B to locate near its supplier, A. The second would measure the transfer cost incentive for industry A to locate near its source of demand, B. This is an appealing concept and one would like to have such data on physical flows of product, distances, and transportation rates in addition to value flows in order to say whether or not significant economies from spatial juxtaposition are possible. Such data are available for few industries, however, and would be prohibitively difficult to collect for a study of many industries spanning the U.S. The information that an input-output study provides is not very helpful in this regard. The flows in such tables are for establishments at present locations and those firms subject to significant economies in transport costs may have already located at places that reduce transport costs, subject to other locational constraints, when compared with less optimal sites.

Leontieff considered the magnitude of a flow between one industry and another to be significant to the first industry in some sense if the flow was greater than 1/nth of the total of all such flows, where n is the number of industries in the economy [28: 12,13]. Richter adopted this same definition of a significant flow which is referred to as a linkage or link. According to their definitions, industry A is said to be linked to B in demand if B demands more of A's total output than 1/nth of the total output of A, where n is the number of industries. Thus a demand linkage indicates that industry A depends upon B as a market. A supply linkage, indicating that A depends upon B as a supplier, exists if A purchases more than 1/nth of its inputs from B. The quantities that industry A sells to, or purchases from, B may also be compared to 1/nth of B's total output and total inputs to determine whether or not B is linked to A in supply or demand.

The way in which linkages are identified according to these definitions, using the notation of the previous chapter, is indicated below:

m = the number of intermediate industries (industrial sectors)

If $Y_{i,j} > \dfrac{1}{m} \sum_{j} Y_{i,j}$, i has a demand link to j

If $Y_{i,j} > \dfrac{1}{m} \sum_{i} Y_{i,j}$, j has a supply link to i

If $Y_{j,i} > \dfrac{1}{m} \sum_{i} Y_{j,i}$, j has a demand link to i

If $Y_{j,i} > \dfrac{1}{m} \sum_{j} Y_{j,i}$, i has a supply link to j

Czamanski has defined supply linkages somewhat differently. According to his definition, industry j is dependent on industry i if the inputs that industry j purchases from industry i are a large proportion of industry i's *total output* (if $\left[Y_{i,j}/\Sigma_j Y_{i,j} \right]$ > some arbitrary value) [9: 139]. It would seem more meaningful to measure the relative importance of a supplier by the proportion of *intermediate inputs* he supplies as was done above rather than by the proportion of *total output* as Czamanski has done.

In a sufficiently disaggregated input-output study, many sectors do not trade at all with many others. The greater the degree of disaggregation, the more pronounced this effect will be. It seems to the present author that it might be more relevant to identify a linkage as above except for letting m be the number of industries with which each given industry actually trades inputs or outputs. Thus, instead of simply dividing total intermediate output or input by the same number in every instance to establish a critical level, there would be two different numbers (one for outputs and one for inputs) for each industry. Otherwise one could be forced to say that all of the industries that one particular industry actually trades with are linked to it when doing so would not be intuitively appealing. For example, suppose that industry A sells its total output of 10 to five other industries as follows: 6, 1, 1, 1, 1. If there are more than 10 sectors in the economy, then A will be said to be linked to each of the five with which it trades rather than only to the one to which it sells 6 as is the case when the recommended procedure for identifying linkages is adopted. It is recognized that his procedure does not eliminate the possible identification of links to all trading industries (consider the previous example with the output distributed as 2, 2, 2, 2, 2), but such identification is considerably reduced, and then is restricted to cases when the linkage is more substantial in a relative sense. In a highly disaggregated input-output table the number of sectors, which is normally used as the divisor in determining which flows are links, is so large that the proposition that such flows are locationally significant for firms in any industry must be questioned. For example, the 1963 Input-Output Study, used in this study, has 363 sectors. To propose that a flow of product in excess of 1/363 of the total output or input of any industry is locationally significant would seem unreasonable. Note that any flow, no matter how small, could become a link by Leontieff's definition, if the number of industries is increased sufficiently.

Any procedure which identifies a linkage whenever an industry trades with another at more than an average level (whether the average is over all, or only over some, sectors) may be inherently limited by the fact that an average or mean is an arbitrary criterion. A measure based on a level of trade more deliberately selected than one which uses the mean level as a significant point in identifying linkages might be preferred but the problem of not knowing the distribution for interindustry flows arises. If the distribution of flows for every industry with all others was known, some points other than the mean could be chosen as significant in identifying linkages. In the present study distributions for inter-industry flows are not computed and the mean and other somewhat arbitrary values will be utilized.

Although Richter intended to consider only those flows intermediate between a producer and his consumers other than the various final demand sectors (specifically, only flows to other manufacturing industries) and exclusive of values added, he apparently divided final output of each industry by the total number of sectors in the 1958 input-output study (86) to obtain a value that he could use to separate significant from insignificant flows [41: 22]. The procedure used in the present study follows Richter's intention and uses flows relative to the flows only to other manufacturing sectors to identify linkages (flows to final demand are utilized to identify industries that are potentially market oriented and flows from primary resources extractors identify potentially material oriented industries). In addition, zero flows are disregarded as recommended above.

Leontieff and Richter did not utilize the full range of variation in flows between industries; Leontieff dichotomized all industries into those that are not linked and those that are linked while Richter only subdivided the latter category into three additional categories based on the size of a linkage for part of his analysis. Richter's three ranges for the percentage of total output represented by the flows between two industries were 1.16% to 3.00%, 3.00% to 7.49% and 7.50% and over. The lower value is simply the limiting value for defining a linkage (or 1/86 because Richter used an 86 sector input-output table). The higher value, 7.5, was chosen because it places most industries usually thought to be first stage resource users into the category on the basis of the percentage of inputs purchased from extractive industries as described above. The intermediate value was chosen to subdivide the range from 1.16 to 7.5.

Richter referred to flows representing more than 7.5% of total inputs or outputs as strong links [41: 80]. The value of 7.5 was chosen only because it was also the figure used to classify industries according to resource use. A better procedure might be to examine the distribution of output in each industry or groups of industries to find an appropriate level. However, for lack of these distributions as well as for comparative purposes, the 7.5 figure is utilized in the present study. It is possible that the procedures outlined for identifying links and strong links in this study may produce a result indicating strong links where there are no weak links. Returning to the example above where an industry distributed its output of 10 to five other industries as 6, 1, 1, 1, and 1, strong links to each of the five would be identified ($1 > .075 \times 10$) while only one link would exist ($6 > .2 \times 10$; $1 < .2 \times 10$).[20]

Streit also measured the strength of linkage between two industries but did not attempt to categorize pairs of industries as being strongly or weakly linked and simply used as a measure of linkage strength the value of

$$L_{i,j} = 1/4[Y_{i,j}(1/\Sigma_j Y_{i,j} + 1/\Sigma_i Y_{i,j}) + Y_{j,i}(1/\Sigma_i Y_{j,i} + 1/\Sigma_j Y_{j,i})].^{[21]}$$

This measure has the value of reducing four relationships for each pair of industries to a single measure. But, in avoiding the establishing of boundaries for various types of linkages, it does not permit the testing of dichotomous hypotheses regarding the effects of the strengths of linkages on industrial location. Streit recognized that a simple average of the four ratios is arbitrary but justified it by noting that there is no empirical evidence indicating that any one of the four links is locationally more significant than the others.[22] Streit's reason for using an average rather than simply the sum was not specified. The sum is utilized in the regression analysis of Chapter 4.

Some authors, such as Hoover, perhaps unjustly criticize the use of input-output studies in location analysis because this use 'assumes that the attraction operates in only one direction; namely that the selling industry A is attracted towards the buying industry B but not the other way around' [19: 11]. The works of both Richter and Streit indicate that this is not true, that the attraction operates in both directions and that input-output analysis is unbiased in this regard.

Results of the investigation of linkages are summarized below in Table 3–3 and in more detail in Appendix Section C–1. Table 3–3 reports the number of linkages found, using both the total number of sectors (as suggested by Leontieff) and the number of nonzero output or input flows as described above. Note that considerably fewer links were identified using the latter, stronger criterion.[23] Links indicating the potential for transportation cost reductions by spatial juxtaposition of manufacturing firms were found for industries identified above as market oriented, material

Table 3–3. Summary of findings with respect to linkages.

	Number[a]
Demand links	1176 (2483)
Strong demand links	428
Supply links	1410 (2203)
Strong supply links	243
Total demand & supply links .	2586 (4686)

a. Numbers in parentheses were derived using the total number of sectors as suggested by Leontieff: others were derived using the number of nonzero flows.

oriented, potentially labor oriented, and not oriented to any of these. The number of links per industry was found to be significantly higher among the latter two groups, suggesting that agglomerative economy oriented industries are more likely to be found among these than among the market or material oriented industries. This result may be viewed as evidence supporting the criteria used to identify market and material orientations.

Examination of all links between individual pairs of industries could be quite revealing. For example, if A is linked to B in supply and/or demand, but B is not linked to A then one might conclude that A is dependent upon B but B is not dependent upon A to the same extent. Such an investigation is beyond the scope of the present study, because of the large number of linkages.

SUMMARY

This chapter has discussed randomness in the location of manufacturing industries and failed to find any randomly located industries with the measure used. Potential orientation to low-wage labor markets was found for 51 industries. Orientation to final demand markets was found for 36 industries and to sources of raw materials for 28 industries. Of the 199 industries, 87 were found to have none of these orientations. The method of identifying potential agglomerative economies using linkages, which indicate the potential for transportation cost reductions, has also been developed. A large number of these potential economies was found among the 199 industries. The next chapter will develop the measure used to identify geographic associations between manufacturing industries. Chapter 5 will then analyze the extent to which potential agglomerative economies have produced agglomerative orientations.

NOTES

1. If such economies exist in significant magnitude, and there is evidence that they may in many industries, at least some firms in industries subject to these economies should have located so as to take advantage of reduced costs dependent upon geographic concentration, either in the form of single large firms or groups of many firms. Otherwise the assumption that a substantial number of firms are economically motivated in choosing locations is questionable. See standard literature regarding the shape of long-run cost curves.
2. This procedure follows that suggested by Bos [4: 46].
3. Such characteristics have been used in other studies (cf. Spiegelman [44]), but the present author felt that the time and effort necessary to adequately integrate such factors into the analysis could not be justified. However, contrary to a priori expectations, land area was found not to be correlated with either regional population or employment. Thus its use would not have biased results as was expected before the correlations were calculated.

4. The estimated employment for each industry in each region for the present study was based on median numbers of employees in only seven plant employee size classes for all industries in the entire U.S. as explained in Chapter 2. Thus it was expected a priori that the number of different minimum sizes would be significantly smaller than the number of industries because each minimum size could only be a weighted sum of the median values.

5. Greenhut has detailed reservations regarding the use of this ratio but these reservations apply only to cases of regional differences in productivity within industries and not to the use of the ratio for interindustry comparisons using aggregate U.S. data [15:320–326]. Isard has advocated use of 'average labor cost per dollar of output' or other measures more difficult to compute [22: 245]. The measure selected here would seem to reflect approximately the same characteristics and, being more readily available and more easily computed, is thought to be adequate for the purpose of this study.

6. The ratio of value added to wages for each industry is published by the Department of Commerce in *Industry Profiles* [54].

7. See Isard [22: 361] and Lichtenberg [29: 265] for examples of industries that may be labor oriented.

8. In this study final demand is interpreted as household final demand or personal consumption expenditures (sector 96.60 in the 1963 Input-Output Study) [56]. The 'final demand' sector in the 1963 Input-Output Study (sector 99.02) includes sales to governments at all levels, investment expenditures and net exports. Clearly the concept of market orientation is not closely related to these latter sectors. As an example of the distinction between the two 'final demands' consider an industry such as number 124, Construction Machinery (SIC #3531), which sells more than seventy-five percent of its output to Input-Output sector 99.02 ('final demand') but sells no output at all to households (sector 96.90). The explanation is simply that most construction machinery goes into investment (sector 96.70) with the remainder being exported or purchased by government.

9. The possibility that population density (a variable used by Spiegelman) rather than population could be a better measure of the market was considered but rejected. Dividing by land area can be viewed as diluting population. Population and industry both tend to be concentrated in and around major cities within regions having large populations, but the geographic size of these regions is determined by political boundaries thus making region-wide density measures inappropriate.

10. Fuchs finds that while 'no industry determines its location without giving some consideration to markets, ... for the great majority of American manufacturing industries the availability of raw materials, labor, transportation and power are usually more important considerations' [14: 152]. He agrees that the distribution of those industries that are market-oriented tends to conform to the distribution of population, however.

11. Czamanski identified urban orientation of industries by correlating population and employment only [8: 187]. He apparently missed the problem mentioned above.

12. Richter classified an industry as market oriented if sales to final demand sectors exceeded 7.5% of total output [41: 90–91]. The figure chosen was simply the same one used in classifying industries according to resource use. It placed 23 of his 51 industrial sectors in the market oriented category. The dual criterion approach is believed to be better justified as indicated above. In Table 3–1 those industries which Richter's criterion would have identified as market oriented are indicated by an asterisk next to their entries in column 3.

13. See Duncan [11: 200–205] and Perloff *et al.* [38: 677ff.] for examples of this broader interpretation.

14. He also used the figure 7.5% to identify second stage resource users but without any substantive justification and, as indicated above, he used the same percentage for market orientation [41: 91].

15. Potential material orientation is thus identified when $S_i = X_{S,i}/X_i > .075$, where $X_{S,i}$ is the value of inputs purchased from primary resource extractors.

16. It would have been preferable to have identified material orientation using the geographic association between a potentially material oriented industry, as indicated by the percentage of inputs obtained from a primary resource extractor, and the primary

resource extractor. The necessary limitation on the number of industries used precluded calculation of such geographic associations, however.

17. A section in Chapter 5 on industrial complexes outlines a procedure used by Czamanski [9] which could be used to identify industries which have input-output structures that are sufficiently alike to possibly produce significant agglomerative economies if firms in these industries locate near to each other even if they do not trade with each other. The regression analysis of Chapter 5 uses a measure of general agglomerative or urbanization economies to account for part of any agglomerative forces not attributable to transport cost reductions on inputs and outputs. Marcus [32] has suggested identifying agglomerative economies for individual regions based on the difference between an actual growth rate and one that might be expected using an export base or shift-share approach. In addition to its inherent defects for a single region and the fact that it lumps together all the different types of agglomerative economies discussed in Chapter 1, such a procedure was not feasible in this study because of the cost of performing the analysis with a large number of regions.

18. While it is true to a certain extent that 'the basic measurement problem is the fact that agglomeration economies are external to individual establishments and do not appear in the books of any firms or the records of any municipality' [46: 11] it is possible to measure potential agglomerative economies using input-output value flows.

19. See Streit [47: 179] for another statement of the problem.

20. The actual results reported in Chapter 5 show that strong links were identified in seven cases where weak links did not exist.

21. Streit's [47] own notation indicated that he used total outputs and inputs for all sectors in the divisors above. It is clear from his explanatory comments that he did not actually do this but used intermediate output instead.

22. Richter confirmed that supply and demand links are equally important in his work [41: 76].

23. Richter found 516 links between the 2550 pairs of industries (a ratio of .203) in his study using the Leontieff definition of a link. Using the same definition, 4686 links between 19701 pairs (a ratio of .238) were found in this study. Thus significantly more (at the .01 level of significance) links were found when the number of industries was increased, and probably not in a meaningful way, as was discussed above. In contrast only 2586 links between the 19701 pairs (a ratio of .131) were found using the revised definition of a link. Average number of links per industry in Richter's study was 10.14 and rose, in this study, to 23.50 with the Leontieff definition but only to 12.45 with the revised definition.

4. The measurement of geographic association

This chapter describes how geographic associations between pairs of industries can be measured systematically. The measure of such associations used in the present study is introduced after reviewing previously-used measures. Variations of the measure with size of employment concentration and between urban and rural regions are then discussed. In the final section associations of more than two industries are commented upon.

The preceding chapter established that firms in some industries probably locate nonrandomly and probably not solely in response to market, material or labor factors and that firms in some of these industries may have locationally significant linkages. Now the extent to which firms tend to associate themselves systematically with each other geographically will be explored. The measure of geographic association between a pair of industries used in the present study is the coefficient of correlation calculated between the proportions of total industry employment found in each of the 377 regions for the two industries. This measure is discussed further after reviewing briefly some other measures that have been used previously.

PREVIOUS MEASURES OF GEOGRAPHIC ASSOCIATION

Richter analyzed most previously-used measures of pairwise geographic association in detail and rejected these for various reasons with which the present author agrees except in the instance indicated below [41: 13–15].[1] To calculate his measure, Richter himself first found the ratio of employ-

ment in industry, i, in region, j, to the population of region j, or $R_{ij} = \dfrac{X_{ij}}{P_j}$

for all industries. His measure of association was then the coefficient of correlation calculated between these ratios for pairs of industries taken over all regions, or r_{ik} between R_{ij} and R_{kj} $(j = 1, \ldots, n)$. Deflating employment by population or any other base in the ratios correlated causes the correlation coefficient measuring the degree of geographic association between two industries to vary with a redistribution of the base even when the redistribution does not affect the employment in the two industries in any way. Sample data illustrating this variation are in Table 4–1.

Table 4–1. Comparison of results of using different measures of geographic association

Sample estimated employment data:

Region number	Industry 1	Industry 6	All industries	All industries redistributed
26	289	1587	87692	97692
34	4903	4332	453288	403288
35	804	2177	74137	84137
36	856	2175	157446	187446
77	158	1264	63500	43500
185	43	224	5365	8365
235	18	112	12546	17546
260	24	658	11534	21534
303	0	123	1022	2022
352	6	60	1108	2108
Totals	7101	12712	867638	867638

Results:

	Measure used	Richter's measure	Richer's measure (with redistribution)
Value of r	.8924	− .4139	− .4001
Value of t	5.5960	−1.2862	−1.2348

Listed in Table 4–1 are estimated employment in industries 1 and 6 for a sample of ten regions and the total industrial employment for those regions (used here as the base for the ratios to be correlated in computing Richter's measure). Also listed is a column showing the total employment in the ten regions arbitrarily redistributed among them. For example 10,000 employees were added to regions 26 and 35, and 20,000 were subtracted from region 77. Below the sample data columns are the coefficients of correlation calculated using the measure proposed for this study, to be explained in the following section, Richter's measure, and Richter's measure using the arbitrarily redistributed total regional employment figures to deflate industry employment in the ratios correlated. This arbitrary redistribution causes a change in the value of the coefficient of correlation. In this case the change is not large, but the example clearly shows that Richter's measure is not invariant under shifts in the base *not* affecting employment in either industry. The measure used in this study is invariant under such redistributions, and this is one of its advantages.

Czamanski proposed an interesting means of identifying geographic associations [8: 187–191]. The method relies on a X^2 test for each pair of industries with the data generated from a 2×2 contingency table based on the following observations:

	Industry k present	Industry k not present
Industry i present	Number of regions with k, i	Number of regions with i only
Industry i not present	Number of regions with k only	Number of regions without i or k

Values of X^2 significantly different from zero imply a geographic association. A distinct disadvantage of this method is that it fails to utilize the level
of an industry's presence in a region in any way; the measures described
above and the one proposed below make use of the level of an industry's
presence in different regions. Czamanski's method would be particularly
inappropriate for use with highly aggregated industrial data (such as is
available at the two- or three-digit SIC level) because aggregation almost
ensures the presence of every industry in every region.

THE MEASURE OF ASSOCIATION USED

Streit [47] used the simple correlation coefficient computed between
regional employment figures as a measure of geographic association as
suggested by McCarty, Hook and Knos [34]. The measure appears in
Appendix Section B–1 where it is also discussed further. Richter criticized
this measure because of an upward bias introduced by the high correlation
between employment and population figures for 51 industries over the 57
SMSA's that he used, and therefore he deflated by population. Such an
upward bias is far less likely with more disaggregated data utilizing non-
SMSA data as well as SMSA data such as those used in the present study.
   The coefficient of correlation between regional employment and population for each industry was reported above in Table 3–1. As can be seen
there, the correlations are not uniformly high. In most cases, the high
correlations are accompanied by a linkage to the final demand sector thus
identifying the industry as market oriented. In the present study then there
is only a small chance of identifying an industry as agglomeration oriented
when it is actually market oriented as can happen with Richter's measure.
   In the present study this measure of Streit [47] and McCarty, Hook and
Knos [34] is used. It avoids the previously mentioned problem associated
with deflating employment figures by population and is not subject to the
large upward bias found by Richter because of the disaggregated nature
of the data from a more extensive set of regions.
   Table 4–1's example of Richter's measure and the one used here high-
lights a dilemma in choosing between the two measures. Examination of
the estimated employment data for the two industries might lead one to

expect some degree of positive geographic association. Calculation of the measure used here gives a value of .89 which may be high because of the high correlation in the sample between estimated employment for each industry and total regional employment or population for each industry. However, calculation of Richter's measure yields a negative value which seems intuitively to be misleading.[2] The present study partially corrects for these defects with the measure chosen and also by requiring the value of the correlation coefficient to be larger than Richter required his to be before considering an association to be significant. In Table 4–1 the correlation between regional employment estimates and regional population is higher for the sample data than for most industries in the study so that the negative aspects of the measure used in this study are overemphasized in the example.

The significance of negative coefficients of geographic association should be considered. The discussion in this study does not utilize agglomerative diseconomies. These could exist if firms in one industry are labor oriented and if regional wage levels rise whenever a second industry is present; then firms in the first industry might avoid locating near firms in the second. It seems more likely, however, that negative coefficients result from pairs of industries having opposite positive orientations, such as market and material orientation as explained above. In this study negative correlations are treated the same as insignificant positive correlations.

Another way of viewing the way in which the measure used here differs from Richer's is as a substitution of total employment in an industry for the population of the region as the divisor in the ratios to be correlated, or the ratios here are $R_{ij} = \dfrac{X_{ij}}{\Sigma_j X_{ij}}$ while Richter's ratios are: $\dfrac{X_{ij}}{P_j}$.[3] One reason for the substitution of industry employment for regional population in the above measure is a belief on the part of the author that the geographic association of industries is related to the relative level of operation of industries at various locations. Richter's measure utilized the relative importance of an industry to a region, whereas the measure used here utilizes the level at which an industry is present in a region relative to its average national presence.[4] A hypothesis which requires an extension of the concept of industry level as being significant, and which states that below some threshold level a specific industry has no locational attraction for another, is examined in the following section.

The ratios used here have previously been utilized as the numerators of ratios known as location quotients which measure the concentration of an industry in a particular region. A location quotient is calculated as:

$$\frac{X_{ij}}{\Sigma_j X_{ij}} \bigg/ \frac{\Sigma_i X_{ij}}{\Sigma_i \Sigma_j X_{ij}}.$$

Because the denominators for location quotients for every industry in a region are identical, one could say that the ratios being correlated are actually location quotients. Richter's measure is more closely related to measures that attempt to identify the degree to which a region specializes in or is dependent upon a particular industry.

A correlation coefficient here, as in Richter, Streit, and McCarty *et al.*, is the measure of association: r_{ik} = correlation coefficient between R_{ij} and R_{kj} calculated over all regions (j). The measure used corrects for another possible defect which Richter admitted remained in his measure [41: 25]. When the ratios correlated are employment as a proportion of regional population, small outputs in small regions are weighted as heavily as large outputs in large regions. The measure used here utilizes proportions with a constant rather than a varying base [41: 25].

Kuh and Meyer pointed out that spurious correlations may arise when the data correlated are ratios. Richter had to consider such a possibility because with his measure he was dividing one series by another series extraneous to the hypotheses to be tested. In the present case the ratios themselves are the subject of the hypothesis and all have a common base, both of which eliminate the need for considering the possibility of spurious correlation according to Kuh and Meyer [26: 401-402].

A growing body of recent literature has called attention to the possible existence and consequences of, and means of dealing with, spatial auto-correlation as an analog of the problem of time series autocorrelation.[5] Spatial autocorrelation is not a concern in the present study, however. Standard econometrics text books show that autocorrelation does not bias estimates of regression coefficients [24: 179]. Because causal ordering is not specified in the relationship between the two industries in the present context, one could calculate either

$$R_{ij} = B_0 + B_1 R_{kj}$$

or

$$R_{kj} = B'_0 + B'_1 R_{ij}$$

and both B_1 and B_1 would be unbiased estimates. Thus the correlation coefficient which is used as the measure of geographic association in this study is also unbiased because it can be calculated as a combination of two unbiased measures:

$$r_{ik} = \sqrt{B_1 B'_1} \; [59: 455].$$

In a later section where additional properties of regression models are used and the estimated regression coefficients are tested for significance, one might be concerned about autocorrelation except for the fact that the disturbance terms in those regressions have neither spatial nor time subscripts. The variables have already summarized all geographic variation.[6]

In previous studies where the industries utilized were more highly aggregated and/or only data from large metropolitan areas were used, it was more probable that each industry appeared in most regions at some non-zero level. In the present study, however, the use of more disaggregated industries and a set of regions completely spanning the country makes it improbable that all, or even most, industries will be present in each region. In fact, among the 199 industries used, the number of regions in which each appears ranges from a low of 8 (in the case of industry 91, SIC 3332, primary lead) to a high of 368 (in the case of industry 6, SIC 2026, fluid milk) with a mean of 86 and a standard error of 120. The distribution for the number of regions in which each industry appears is given in Appendix Table B–3. Some statistical consequences of utilizing data containing a large number of zero observations are examined in Appendix Section B–1. As recommended there, paired zero observations were omitted from calculations of correlation coefficients measuring the strengths of geographic associations in this study.

The 19701 coefficients of correlation between all different pairs of the 199 industries were calculated and the resulting distribution was examined in an aggregate fashion with the use of frequency counts for coefficients falling in various magnitude intervals. On the basis of this examination it was decided that significant values of the correlation coefficient should identify pairs of industries with more than a merely statistically significant degree of association. While Richter considered any coefficient of correlation significantly greater than zero to indicate a geographic association between two industries, the present study identifies a locationally significant geographic association only when the coefficient is significantly greater than 0.5. Even using this much stronger criterion for identifying significant geographic associations, 1040 such associations were found (this represents 5.28% of all possible associations). The results for individual industries are summarized in Appendix Section C–1. As can be seen there, the number of associations for an industry ranges from 0 (for 89 industries) to 64 (for industry 70, Miscellaneous Plastics Products).

THE EFFECT OF CLUSTER SIZE ON GEOGRAPHIC ASSOCIATION

A hypothesis of the present study mentioned in Chapter 1 is that the geographic location of some industries will influence the location of others to which they are linked only when sufficiently large clusters of the first are present in a region.[7] This would be the case if a first industry is a major supplier of a second, but clusters of the first will be less likely to influence locations in the second if the clusters are not large enough to supply the quantity of product demanded as an input to a single cluster of the second. This factor underlies the previously discussed correlations between pro-protions of industries in regions. The difference here is that a threshold size for influencing the locations of other industries is postulated. For individuals or groups interested in regional development, especially in smaller regions, it is important to know, if possible, whether it is merely a given industry or if a large cluster of that industry is necessary to be loca-tionally significant for clusters of another industry. This effect was not identified in the previous correlations between proportions of industries in regions.

The effect of threshold size is investigated by subdividing each member of a randomly selected set of ten sample industries into three categories based on size of employment estimates. The regional employment distribu-tion for each category is then correlated with the regional employment distribution for each of the other 29 categories and the results are examined to see whether or not there appear to be any significant threshold size effects.

Theoretically a threshold size, if one exists, might be found by correlating the proportions of an industry present with proportions of a second indus-try only in regions where the second industry is present at greater than a hypothesized threshold level. The hypothesized threshold level could be varied until it was just large enough to produce a significant correlation or until it was determined that none existed. The computational requirements of such a procedure are too great to make it feasible in the present study. A second possible procedure for identifying the threshold size for clusters of firms in an industry to influence the locations of clusters in another would be to use multiple regression analysis with dummy variables repre-senting various possible threshold sizes. The smallest size for which a significant regression coefficient was found could then be designated as the threshold size for one industry vis-à-vis locations of clusters in a second. Again the computational requirements exceed the feasible range for the present study, and the procedure described above and in more detail below is used.

For the analysis, the sample of ten industries was randomly selected to include pairs of industries which are significantly associated with each other in the aggregate and pairs which are not; it also includes pairs of industries with significant linkages and pairs without. The employment estimates by region for each of the ten industries were divided into three groups, based on the size of the estimated employment. For a given industry the small size category includes all regional employment estimates smaller than the minimum regional employment size for the industry plus 5% of the difference between the minimum and the maximum size for the industry.[8] The medium category includes all estimates larger than the minimum size for the industry by amounts betwen 5% and 10% of the difference between the minimum and maximum size for the industry. The large category includes all larger estimates. Thus from each original industry, three new categories were constructed. For each region only one category could have a nonzero entry for a given industry. If the original estimated employment figure for a region was allocated to the small category, both the medium and large categories would have a zero recorded for that region.

The correlation coefficient used as the measure of geographic association was then calculated for every pair among the 30 industries. It was expected that correlation coefficients involving the larger clusters in an industry would be found to be larger more often than those involving the smaller clusters. The expectation was derived, in part, directly from the threshold size concept. In addition, empirical observation indicates that larger clusters for many manufacturing industries are frequently located in large (in terms of total employment) regions where more generalized agglomerative economies are stronger and where specific linkages to third industries are more likely to occur.[9]

Because each of the industries in the sample is correlated with each of the others at three levels, nine correlation coefficients are produced for each pair of the ten aggregate industries in addition to the one previously obtained for the pair in the aggregate. These appear in Appendix Table C-3 in the following format:

	Industry$_{kS}$	Industry$_{kM}$	Industry$_{kL}$
Industry$_{iS}$	$r_{iS,kS}$	$r_{iS,kM}$	$r_{iS,kL}$
Industry$_{iM}$	$r_{iM,kS}$	$r_{iM,kM}$	$r_{iM,kL}$
Industry$_{iL}$	$r_{iL,kS}$	$r_{iL,kM}$	$r_{iL,kL}$

Perhaps the most significant result of this analysis is the lack of any discernible consistent pattern of variation among the nine correlation coefficients for each of the 45 pairs of industries in the sample. The hypothesis of larger coefficients for pairs of large subindustries is not supported completely. In over half of the sample cases, another of the nine coefficients was larger than $r_{iL,kL}$.[10] In all such cases, however, no coefficient was locationally significant as this term was defined above. In all cases where the two aggregate industries had a locationally significant coefficient of correlation, $r_{iL,kL}$ was the largest of the nine coefficients and in no case was any coefficient other than $r_{iL,kL}$ found to be large enough to be considered locationally significant. These results indicate that when a significant association exists between two industries that it is the larger units in each that are producing the association. This might be an example of a marginal cost consideration only affecting the behavior of the largest firms, which may be the most cost conscious. Thus there is some support for the threshold size effect on geographic association. Certainly the small sample and crude method used here do not yield results that permit unequivocal rejection of the hypothesis of such an effect.

VARIATION IN THE MEASURE OF GEOGRAPHIC ASSOCIATION BETWEEN URBAN AND RURAL REGIONS

Some advantages of using data for non-SMSA regions as well as for SMSA's were detailed above in Chapter 2. Czamanski found that the effect of several locational factors varies with size of cities for some industries [8: 195]. The hypothesis that industrial location behavior with respect to geographic associations of clusters of firms in different industries differs between SMSA and non-SMSA regions can be tested by calculating the correlation coefficient which measures geographic association for a sample of industries separately for SMSA and non-SMSA regions. The calculations are performed for only a sample of industries because the expense of calculating and analyzing an additional 39402 correlation coefficients was not felt to be justified in the present study. The sample of 15 industries includes the ten used in the investigation of the effect of threshold size plus five additional randomly selected industries. The resulting calculations are summarized in Appendix Table C–4.

Inspection of the distribution of estimated employment by regions indicates clearly that larger employment clusters are generally located in SMSA's and smaller ones in non-SMSA regions. The discussion regarding threshold size in the preceding section would lead one to expect larger coefficients of correlation for industry pairs in SMSA's. The results support this expectation: for 97 of 105 industry pairs the coefficient of correlation is larger for the SMSA's than for the non-SMSA regions. The fact that the measure of geographic association is significantly different for almost every pair of industries between the SMSA and non-SMSA regions indicates that the behavior measured differs in different kinds of regions and that extension of results obtained for one type to another may be erroneous. This conclusion might lead one to expect that the size of the coefficient would also vary between larger and smaller SMSA's (as suggested by Difiglio and Stevens [10]) or over any other partitioning of the set of regions according to size. For this reason, the measure which best captures the essence of the behavior of the industry, regardless of location, may be the coefficient of correlation calculated over all regions as is done in this study.

GEOGRAPHIC ASSOCIATIONS AMONG MORE THAN TWO INDUSTRIES

A logical extension of the preceding analysis of the geographic association between two industries is the analysis of geographic association among three, four or more industries. Spatial relationships involving more than two industries can be described with the aid of higher order correlation coefficients as suggested by Streit [47: 183]. Coefficients of multiple correlation can describe the degree of association between one industry and any group of others. Partial correlation coefficients can be used to describe the degree of association between groups of industries with the effect of groups of other industries removed. Partial correlation coefficients might have been used in the preceding sections also but were not because of the magnitude of the computations necessary to obtain such coefficients. While computation of partial correlation coefficients from simple correlation coefficients is theoretically straightforward, when large numbers of simple correlation coefficients are involved the computations become cumbersome if not prohibitively complex. For example, while the partial correlation between industries 1 and 2 with the effects of industry 3 removed is simply

$$r_{12.3} = \frac{r_{12} - r_{13}r_{23}}{\sqrt{(1 - r_{13}{}^2)(1 - r_{23}{}^2)}}$$

the partial correlation between 1 and 2 with the effects of industries 3 and 4 removed may be expressed as

$$r_{12.34} = -\frac{C_{12}{}^2}{\sqrt{C_{11}C_{22}}}$$

where the C_{ij} are co-factors of the 4×4 matrix of simple correlation coefficients. Associations of more than two industries are therefore determined in Chapter 5 using the bilateral associations only.

SUMMARY

This chapter has supported the use of the coefficient of correlation computed between regional employment distributions as an appropriate measure of geographic association between pairs of industries. The results of calculating this measure for all pairs of the 199 industries in the present study were presented. Variation in the measure with size of employment concentration was found to be inconsistent with some evidence indicating stronger associations between larger concentrations. Significant variation in the measure between urban and rural regions was found to exist. Computational problems of attempting to measure multilateral associations were summarized. The next chapter will explore the impact of the locational factors described in Chapter 3 on industrial location in the form of geographic associations as described in this chapter.

NOTES

1. Richter did not review the work of Czamanski [8] discussed below.
2. Richter found a large number of negative correlations in his study (over half of all such coefficients were negative) but did not comment on these [41: 26]. In the present study negative correlations are treated as 0 as discussed further below.
3. Note that the correlation between $\dfrac{X_{ij}}{\Sigma_j X_{ij}}$ and $\dfrac{X_{kj}}{\Sigma_j X_{kj}}$ is identical to the correlation between X_{ij} and X_{kj} because $\Sigma_j X_{ij}$ and $\Sigma_j X_{kj}$ are constants for all observations. The discussion here is in terms of the ratios, however, to emphasize the difference between the measure used and Richter's.
4. Another ratio, which has not been used elsewhere, is the ratio of regional industry employment to total regional employment. This measure was used in the example of Table 4–1 and is subject to the same criticisms as Richer's measure.
5. McCamely [33] provides a clear statement of the problem and lists other related work.
6. It is fortunate that the problem of spatial autocorrelation does not have to be dealt with in the present study. Means of correcting for autocorrelation proposed to date utilize distances between points and relative compass directions (or geographic coordinates) both of which would be prohibitively difficult to obtain for the present study. For example, if the geographic centers for each of the 377 regions were already known (and they are not), then there would be 70,876 distances to calculate.
7. According to Isard, 'it is fully recognized that spatial-juxtaposition economies ... are closely interrelated with the scales of the activities ...' [22: 405]. Czamanski states 'that as an element of industrial location, size of plant is second in importance only to industrial category ...' [8: 185].
8 The range from the minimum to the maximum was originally divided into equal thirds but this resulted in almost all observations being in the small group. Examination of the distributions of employment estimates for all the industries revealed that the lower 5% and next 5% of the range would yield adequate sample sizes for most industries. It would be more desirable to subdivide the clusters in each industry utilizing some characteristics of the distributions of cluster sizes other than the minimum and maximum. Characteristics of the individual distributions are not known, however, and the scope of the present study does not seem to warrant investigation of them. The hypothesis that is to be tested is whether or not size of industry presence in a region is effective in geographic associations. To test this hypothesis, even an arbitrary division may provide sufficient differentiation.
9. Such a finding would be somewhat in conflict with the findings of Difiglio and Stevens to the effect that medium-sized SMSA's can be characterized as industrial complexes while large establishments which are capable of internalizing their services may locate independently in small SMSA's and small establishments are forced to remain in the protective 'seedbed' of large SMSA's. The conflict may be largely resolved if a threshold size effect exists [10: 35].
10. For four of the 45 pairs of industries one of the nine coefficients of subindustry correlation produced a higher value than the positive value for the two aggregate industries. In each of these four cases the larger value did involve the large subindustry for one or both industries.

5. The impact of linkages on industrial location

The objective of this chapter is to analyze the impact of potential agglomerative economies, which arise from reducing transportation costs through spatial juxtaposition of manufacturing industries, and other factors as identified in Chapter 3, on the geographic locations of firms in selected manufacturing industries, as described in Chapter 4. Results from Chapters 3 and 4 are first summarized, integrated and compared with previous results. Particular attention is paid to the relationship of linkages to geographic associations. Regression analysis for a sample of industries is then used to expand the analysis of the impact of linkages and other factors on geographic associations. In the final section of the chapter the identification of industrial complexes is considered.

ANALYSIS OF RESULTS FOR ALL INDUSTRIES

Table 5–1 summarizes the findings of Chapters 3 and 4 for the characteristics of the individual industries and pairs of industries. Section I of Table 5–1 essentially summarizes the results reported in Table 3–1; Section II reproduces part of Table 3–3; and Section III summarizes the results reported in Appendix Tables C-3 and C-4. Table 5-2 integrates the findings with respect to associations described in Chapter 4 with those for linkages and orientations discussed in Chapter 3. The following paragraphs will analyze these and other data in some detail and in comparison with earlier work, especially that of Richter [41]. Geographic associations as possible expressions of the realization of potential agglomerative economies in the form of linkages will be examined first.

The data in Tables 5–1 and 5–2 can be used to comment on the impact of links on associations between industries in the aggregate by comparing the frequencies in Table 5–3 (which is based on Tables 5–1 and 5–2). Table 5–3 shows the joint frequency distributions for pairs of industries in linkage and association dimensions. Looking at the rows of Table 5–3 one can see that a total of 1040 pairs of industries were found to be associated. Each pair is counted twice and the value 2080 appears in the table, however, because the frequency counts for linkages, which can exist from one member of an industry pair to another and not the reverse, do not distinguish

Table 5-1. Summary of individual characteristic findings.

	Basis for number reported	Number	(%)
I. Orientation of 199 industries	Total number of industries	199	(100.0)
A. Random	Distribution of total employment	0	(0.0)
B. Labor (potentially)	Value added per dollar of wages	51	(25.6)
C. Market	Proportion of output sold to final demand & correlation of population & employment .	36	(18.1)
D. Material	Proportion of inputs bought from resource extractors & correlation of population & employment	28	(14.1)
E. Other[a]		87	(43.7)
II. Links for industry pairs	Total potential linked pairs	79102[b]	(100.0)
A. All links	Interindustry flows	2586	(3.3)
B. Strong links	Distribution of large flows . . .	671	(0.9)
C. Weak links	Distribution of significant flows	1922	(2.4)
D. Demand links	Distribution of output	1176	(1.5)
E. Supply links	Distribution of inputs	1410	(1.8)
III. Associations between industry pairs	Total number of pairs	19701[c]	(100.0)
A. Significant associations	Correlation between employment proportions	1040	(5.3)
B. Urban-rural pairs	Industry pairs in 15 sample industries	105	(100.0)
1. Pairs associated in all regions	Correlation in all regions	29	(27.6)
2. Associated in urban regions only	Correlation in urban regions . .	30	(28.6)
3. Associated in rural regions only	Correlation in rural regions . . .	3	(2.9)
C. Threshold size pairs	Industry pairs in 10 sample industries	45	(100.0)
1. Associated, whole industries	Correlation for all concentrations	15	(33.3)
2. Associated, large size for each	Correlation for largest concentration	10	(22.2)
3. Associated, other sizes for either	Correlation with smaller concentration	0	(0.0)

a. Appendix Table C-2 shows that 67 industries have both linkages and geographic associations with second industries and thus might be identified as agglomerative economy oriented. Many of these also fall into other categories, however. In addition, many have more than one other industry with which both linkage and association relationships exist. For these reasons and the fact that this entire chapter examines the impact of linkages on associations, agglomerative oriented industries are not listed separately.

b. Total potential links is 79102 because each industry can be linked to all others, including itself in both supply and demand ($2 \times 199 \times 199 = 79102$).

c. Each industry can be pared with 198 others, but because the measure of geographic association of industry i and industry k is identical to the association of k and i there are only 19701 different associations ($199 \times 198/2 = 19701$). The association of an industry with itself is not considered because it would always be perfect whereas an industry may, or may not, be linked to itself.

Source: Tables 3-1, 3-3 and Appendix Tables C-2, C-3, and C-4.

Table 5–2. Integration of orientation, linkage and association findings.

Orientation (1)	Number of industries (2)	Number of links[a] (3)	Number of associations[b] (4)	Number of associations accompanied by links[c] (5)
Labor (potential)	51	509	557	54
Market	36	159	644	25
Material	28	124	11	3
Other	87	764	871	98
Total	202	1556	2083	180
Adjusted total[d]	199	1545	2080	180
Strong link to final demand[e]	68	341	753	44
None	131	1204	1327	136
Total	199	1545	2080	180

a. The number of links here refers to the number of *second industries* to which industries falling into the classification listed in the left-hand column are linked. The linkage may be in demand, supply, strong demand and/or strong supply. The linked industries may be in the same classification or another.
b. The number of associations refers to the number of second industries with which industries falling into the classification listed in the left-hand column have significant geographic associations. Each association is thus counted twice, once for each industry.
c. See footnote c, Table 5–4.
d. Because three industries were classified as both market and material oriented, the unadjusted totals double count the links and associations for these industries.
e. Includes industries which sell more than 7.5% of output to final demand sectors.
Source: Table 5–1 and Appendix Table C–2.

duplicate associations of the duplicate pairs. A total of 180 pairs were found to be linked as well as associated. Looking at the columns, one can see that 1545 pairs of industries were linked, of which 1365 were not also associated. The figures there indicate that linked pairs are more likely to be associated (proportion, $180/1545 = .117$) than nonlinked pairs ($1900/38056 = .050$); and that associated pairs are more frequently accompanied by links ($180/2080 = .087$) than nonassociated pairs

Table 5–3. Comparison of total linkages and associations of industry pairs[a].

	Number of linked pairs	Number of nonlinked pairs	Totals
Number of pairs associated	180 (.005) 117 (.046)	1900 (.048) 255 (.100)	2080 (.053) 372 (.146)
Number of pairs not associated	1365 (.034) 352 (.138)	36156 (.913) 1826 (.716)	37521 (.947) 2178 (.854)
Totals	1545 (.039) 469 (.184)	38056 (.961) 2081 (.816)	39601 (1.00) 2550 (1.00)

a. In each cell of the table Richter's results are below those of the present study. Relative frequencies are in parentheses.
Source: Tables 5–1 and 5–2 and Richter [41].

(1365/37521 = .036). Tests of the difference between these proportions yield t values of 11.51 and 11.52, respectively, both of which are significant at the .01 level of significance. This result supports Richter's conclusion that the aggregate impact of linkages on associations was significant [41: 72]. Because the present study uses stronger criteria in the identification of links and associations, the proportions above are smaller than Richter's but the ratios of the two proportions in each test are similar here to Richter's.

Another way of measuring the aggregate impact of linkages on geographic associations is to compute the coefficient of correlation between the measure of association and a measure of linkage over all pairs of industries. Such a measure has the advantage of using the actual values of both the association and linkage measures rather than using only the number of those which exceed certain somewhat arbitrary values. Streit computed such coefficients for data from France and Germany using the same measure of association as the one used in this study and using the average of the (weak) links between every pair as the measure of linkage (as described in Chapter 3). His values of .13 and .39 for the two countries are considerably larger than the value of .079 computed using a similar method in the present study.[1] The difference can probably best be attributed to differences in the levels of aggregation between Streit's work and the present one. The existence of a significant difference between the coefficient for Germany and France found by Streit might also suggest that there is systematic international variation in the importance of linkages for industrial location. However, the fact that the geographic aggregation used by Streit differed considerably between France and Germany makes direct comparisons of their coefficients difficult [47].

The results discussed in the two preceding paragraphs seem to suggest that links, which are a measure of the potential for reducing transportation costs, have a significant, but not large, impact on the location of industries in the aggregate. A next step is to attempt to ascertain whether or not certain kinds of links are more important than others in the location of industries.

Table 5–4 shows that strong links are accompanied by a significant geographic association in 77 of 671 instances (p_1 = .115) and that weak links are accompanied by an association with a frequency that is not statistically different (p_2 = .118, t, for the difference between p_1 and p_2, is .02). This result contradicts Richter's findings, but the contradiction may be explained by recalling that the criterion for the identification of a weak link in the present study is more stringent than it was for Richter, while the criterion for strong links is the same. Thus one would expect a relatively smaller percentage of weak linkages, identified by a weak criterion, to be

Table 5–4. Integration of demand-supply, Strong-weak linkage findings with geographic association findings.

	Demand links	Supply links	Total
Strong links[a]	428	243	671
Accompanied by associations[b]	52 (.121)	25 (.103)	77 (.115)
Weaks links only	755	1167	1922
Accompanied by associations	86 (.114)	140 (.120)	226 (.118)
Total links	1183	1410	2593
Accompanied by associations	138 (.117)	165 (.117)	303[c] (.117)
Total weak links	1176	1410	2586
Accompanied by associations	136 (.116)	165 (.117)	301 (.116)

a. Strong links occur in conjunction with weak links in all but seven instances.
b. Each figure in parentheses is the proportion of the number of links in the row above that are accompanied by an association.
c. Industry i can be linked to industry k in four ways: (1) demand, (2) supply, (3) strong demand and (4) strong supply. Because there is only one association between the pair, the number of links accompanied by a geographic association can be larger than the number of associations accompanied by one or more links. The latter number is 180 in Tables 5–2 and 5–3 while the former, in this table and Tables 5–5 and 5–6, is 303.
Source: Appendix Table C–2.

accompanied by associations and for the frequency of associations with strong links to be greater in Richter's case. Because the criteria for identifying associations are different in this study and Richter's, the pure effect of the criteria for identifying weak links cannot be observed. Table 5–5 compares the findings of this study with those of Richter for weak and strong links. These results suggest that if the criterion for the identification of a link advocated in this study is accepted then the distinction between weak and strong links is not meaningful. Such a distinction might be meaningful if the criterion for identifying a strong link was made more stringent.

Table 5–5. Comparison of effects of strong and weak linkages[a].

	Number of strong links	Number of weak links	Total
Association	77 (.030)	226 (.087)	303[b](.117)
	19 (.037)	172 (.333)	191 (.369)
No association	594 (.229)	1696 (.654)	2290 (.883)
	42 (.081)	284 (.549)	326 (.631)
Total	671 (.259)	1922 (.741)	2593 (1.00)
	61 (.118)	456 (.882)	517 (1.00)

a. In each cell of the table Richter's results are below those of the present study. Relative frequencies are in parentheses.
b. See footnote c of Table 5–4.
Source: Richter [41] and Table 5–4.

Table 5–6. Comparison of effects of supply and demand linkages[a].

	Supply links	Demand links	Total
Association	165 (.064)	138 (.053)	303[b](.117)
	73 (.141)	58 (.112)	131 (.254)
No association	1245 (.480)	1045 (.403)	2290 (.883)
	213 (.413)	172 (.333)	385 (.796)
Total	1410 (.544)	1183 (.456)	2593 (1.00)
	286 (.554)	230 (.446)	516 (1.00)

a. In each cell of the table Richter's results are below those of the present study. Relative frequencies are in parentheses.
b. See footnote c of Table 5–4.
Source: Table 5–4 and Richter [41].

Table 5–4 also shows that demand links are accompanied by a significant geographic association in 138 of 1183 instances ($p = .117$) and that supply links are accompanied by associations just as frequently (in 165 of 1410 instances, $p = .117$). The conclusion that supply and demand links are equally important for industrial location in the aggregate agrees with Richter's findings in this area. Table 5–6 compares the findings of this study with those of Richter for demand and supply links. Again the differences in relative frequencies is probably attributable to the criteria used for identifying links and associations.

An additional possibility, that the effects of supply and demand links and weak and strong links interact, can be investigated using the data in Table 5–4. Pairwise t tests indicate that the percentages shown in the table are not statistically different from each other and the conclusion is that not only are demand and supply links equally important and differences between weak and strong links insignificant, but these factors do not interact to

Table 5–7. Variation of linkage and association relationships by industry orientation.

Orientation (1)	Number of associations ÷ number of links (2)	Number of associations accompanied by links		
		÷ Number of associations (3)	÷ Number of links (4)	÷ Number of industries (5)
Market	4.050	.039	.157	.694
Material	.089	.273	.024	.107
Labor	1.094	.097	.106	1.059
Other	1.140	.113	.128	1.126
Total	1.346	.087	.117	.905
Final demand	2.208	.058	.129	.647

Source: Table 5–2.

produce differential effects on aggregate industrial location. Thus the distinction among these may not be useful.

Table 5-2 shows figures that provide evidence indicating that the relationship between industrial location and linkages does seem to differ with industries of different orientations as identified in Chapter 3. This variation is most apparent for material and market oriented industries. Table 5-7 shows several ratios calculated from the figures in Table 5-2. Column 2 shows the ratio of the total number of associations (with all other industries) for the industries in the classification in column 1 divided by the total number of links (to all other industries) for the same group of industries. Columns 3, 4 and 5 show the ratio of the number of associations accompanied by a link for the industrial classification in column 1 divided by three different magnitudes. One would not expect material oriented industries to locate near others as frequently as industries in other categories and the results in columns 2, 4 and 5 clearly support this expectation. Significant differences (at the .01 level) between market and material oriented industries exist for all of the ratios shown. This is the result expected because market oriented industries locate near other industries whether they are linked or not.

One might interpret market and material oriented industries as representing, respectively, final and early stages of processing. The figures in Table 5-7, especially for the number of associations accompanied by links as a proportion of the number of links, indicate that links are more important locationally for industries in later rather than earlier stages of processing. Figures for the entire 68 industries that are strongly linked to final demand, rather than just those identified as being market oriented, tend to support the hypothesis further. They are cited here because they provide data more directly related to processing stage than the orientation concepts developed in Chapter 3. Additional support for this hypothesis is provided by the fact that the ratios in Table 5-7 for potentially labor oriented industries and for those industries identified as other oriented (possibly agglomerative economy, as noted above), both of which may be intermediate stage processors, are between those for material and market oriented industries for three of the four ratios. Richter's results also supported the finding that links are more important to later stage processors.[2]

Two additional aspects of Table 5-7 should be commented upon. First, a relatively high proportion of linkage-accompanied associations may exist among the potentially labor oriented industries because a number of these are not actually labor oriented. Chapter 3 explained how the realization of potential orientation was identified for market and material orientation but not for labor orientation. Thus some industries that should be classified as agglomerative economy oriented may be in the labor oriented category. Second, the fact that the importance of linkages for associations among those industries classified as other oriented does not seem to be larger than it is may be because this category may be more likely than any of the others to include random oriented industries which were not successfully identified using the test for nonrandomness of Chapter 3. The similarity of the ratios in Table 5–7 for potentially labor oriented industries and for those with no orientation may be reflecting the heterogeneity of both of these classifications (none of the ratios for the two groups are statistically different at the .10 level of significance).

REGRESSION ANALYSIS OF INDIVIDUAL MANUFACTURING INDUSTRIES

The preceding analysis has produced several tentative conclusions regarding the determinants of variation in the geographic association of industries in the aggregate. The most important conclusion for this study is that agglomerative economies representing reductions in transportation costs through spatial juxtaposition among manufacturing industries do have a significant impact on geographic associations. Furthermore, aggregate association behavior seemed to vary somewhat systematically among industries in the orientation categories previously identified.

For policy purposes, however, knowledge of the locational behavior of individual industries is essential. The data used above are adequate to permit individual industry analysis making use of the measures developed in earlier sections. The individual industry analysis will also illustrate how regression analysis can be used to integrate all of the measures developed above in a single model. Other methods of analyzing individual industries were considered. Richter, for example, examined the impact of linkages on individual industries by computing a correlation between each industry's employment proportion and the proportion of employment in all linked industries over all regions. He compared this figure with a similar correlation between each industry and a random selection of industries, finding that linkages produced a higher average correlation than random industries. A similar analysis was not undertaken in the present study because the regression analysis described below includes variables which permit a more meaningful analysis of the effect of linkages on the location of each industry. The analysis of variance was another framework considered for the examination of individual industries but was rejected because its results would have been similar to those of the regression analysis and, by using the latter, comparisons could be made with another study which used regression analysis.[3]

The following paragraphs describe the regression models employed in this study and the results of applying them to individual industries. Because it was not feasible to present and analyze the results of applying each of the five models described below to all of the 199 industries, a sample of 20 industries was selected. It was felt that more could be learned about industrial associations from applying a number of models to a few industries than from applying one or two models to all industries. The sample of 20 industries includes the 15 used for the analysis of urban-rural differences in geographic association in Chapter 4 plus five additional randomly selected industries. Table 5–8 lists the sample industries and some of their characteristics.

Shown below are the five regression models that will be estimated for the sample industries.

Model 1: $r_{kj} = B_{01} + B_{11}L_{kj} + u_1$.

Model 2: $r_{kj} = B_{02} + B_{12}L_{kj} + B_{22}G_{kj} + u_2$.

Model 3: $r_{kj} = B_{03} + B_{13}L_{kj} + B_{23}M_{kj} + u_3$.

Model 4: $r_{kj} = B_{04} + B_{14}L_{kj} + B_{24}G_{kj} + B_{34}M_{kj} + B_{44}R_{kj} + B_{54}W_{kj} + B_{64}N_{kj} + u_4$

Model 5: $r_{kj} = B_{05} + B_{15}S_{kj} + B_{25}D_{kj} + B_{35}G_{kj} + B_{45}M_{kj} + B_{55}R_{kj} + B_{65}W_{kj} + B_{75}N_{kj} + u_5$

The independent variables appearing in these models are explained in more detail below; the following listing simply indicates the type of variation that each was designed to reflect.

L_{kj}: Average linkage
G_{kj}: Generalized agglomerative economies
M_{kj}: Market orientation
R_{kj}: Material orientation
W_{kj}: Labor orientation
N_{kj}: Random orientation
S_{kj}: Supply linkage
D_{kj}: Demand linkage

In each of the five models the dependent variable is the correlation coefficient, r_{kj}, indicating degree of geographic association between industry k and all other, $j = 1, \ldots, 199, j \neq k$.

Model 1 uses the average linkage value, L_{kj} (described in Chapter 3), as the only explanatory variable. It attempts to explain variation in the geographic associations of one industry with others as a function of only the average value of the measure of the potential agglomerative economies between the first industry and all others. The results of applying this model to each of the 20 sample industries appears in Table 5–9. The R^2 column shows that this model explains very little of the variation in the measure of associ-

Table 5–8. Characteristics of 20 sample industries used in regression analysis.

Industry number	Abbreviated title	Number of regions	Number of associations	Number of links	Number of links with associations	Correlation with all industry	Orientation[a]
6	Fluid milk	368	52	4	1	.872	2
47	Metal household furniture	116	43	3	3	.826	2
61	Plastic materials and resins	135	0	29	0	.397	0
65	Paints and allied products	229	57	27	18	.887	0
70	Miscellaneous plastic products	288	64	38	29	.914	0
114	Metal stampings	220	42	43	14	.827	1
120	Fabricated metal products	224	60	15	4	.883	0
150	Motors and generators	121	0	0	0	.467	1
157	Household laundry equipment	27	0	5	0	.083	0
169	Electronic components	210	51	16	7	.843	1
170	Storage batteries	111	0	5	0	.445	0
178	Aircraft	56	4	3	1	.482	0
188	Mechanical measuring devices	150	13	16	1	.666	0
38	Sawmills and planing mills	334	2	21	2	−.008	1
56	Paperboard mills	126	0	8	0	.236	0
67	Paving mixtures and blocks	236	20	1	0	.732	0
101	Iron and steel forgings	94	4	21	0	.568	1
126	Elevators and moving stairs	63	3	2	0	.355	0
134	Printing trades machinery	97	46	1	1	.785	0
144	Commercial laundry equipment	60	45	0	0	.355	0

a. 0, 1, 2 refer to no identified orientation, labor orientation and market orientation respectively. Unfortunately the selection procedure did not place any industries subsequently identified as material oriented in the sample.
Source: Table 3–1 and Appendix Tables A–5, C–1, C–2 and C–3.

ation for most of the 20 industries (R^2 ranges from .000 to .440). This was expected because the previously reported correlation between each industry pair and the average linkage for the pair was only .079 ($R^2 = .006$). The standard errors of estimate (not shown in the table) were also uniformly high in comparison to the values of the dependent variable. Note, however, that the regression coefficient was found to be significantly greater than zero (at the .10 level of significance or better) for 10 of the 20 industries. Applying this same model to more highly aggregated industries in France and Germany, Streit also found low explanatory power but he found only six significant regression coefficients among his 52 industry equations [47: 180]. This difference in proportion of significant coefficients for the linkage variable is statistically significant (at the .01 level) and could be interpreted as indicating that the linkage variable is more important for associations when less highly aggregated industries are considered.

Model 2 attempts to improve on the explanatory power of Model 1 by introducing an additional variable. On the assumption that industries k and j might each be attracted to a location, in part, by its general agglomerative factors, even if they are not linked, the variable added might be one which indicates the degree to which general agglomerative factors influence the locations of both industry k and industry j. If one assumes that industry, as a whole, adequately represents these general agglomerative factors, the coefficient of correlation, r_{jx}, between employment in all industries together, x, and employment in an individual industry, j, can be used to measure the strength of the general agglomerative factor for j. The variable used in the regression equation can then be the sum or average of the measure of attractiveness of general agglomerative factors for industry j and industry k, or $G_{kj} = 1/2(r_{jx} + r_{kx})$. This was the variable used by Streit and which is also used in Model 2. A difficulty with the variable is that it fails to differentiate between the case of low correlations for both industries and a high correlation for one and a low correlation for the other. For example, the measured value of the variable would be the same if the correlation was .5 for each or if the correlation for one was .99 while the other was .01. Clearly one would expect the general agglomerative factor to increase the size of the measured geographic association between the two industries more in the first case than in the second.

An alternative use of the general agglomerative factor as measured by the correlation, r_{jx}, for each industry is to compute the product of the values for each pair: $G_{kj} = (r_{jx})(r_{kx})$. In the example above, the values for G_{kj} would be .2500 and .0099 providing the desired differentiation. This muliplicative form of the variable, r_x, might be further justified if the r_{jx} values are thought of as relative frequencies with which each industry responds to general agglomerative factors. The product of the two would then represent the relative frequency with which one would expect the response of the two to coincide geographically. The primary reason for using the additive formulation instead is to permit comparisons with Streit's results.

The results for Model 2 for each of the 20 industries are also in Table 5–9. With this model the amount of variation explained is generally high. Note that with Model 2 two values of R^2 are less than the highest value of R^2 with Model 1. The increase in R^2 values, and the reduction in the standard errors of estimate to reasonable magnitudes, is attributable to the high correlation between G and the measure of association for most industries. The regression coefficient for G is highly significant (at the .01 level) for all 20 industries. With the effects of generalized agglomerative economies, G, removed the coefficient for the linkage variable, L, is significantly different from zero for ten industries, the same number for which it was significant in Model 1.[4] That linkages are important for some industries

Table 5-9. Regression results for models 1 and 2[a].

	Model 1		Model 2			
Industry	L	R^2	L	G	R^2	Standard error of estimate
6	−.039	.001	.018	.961***	.922	.064
	(.071)		(.020)	(.020)		
47	.249***	.062	.024	.962***	.937	.067
	(.069)		(.019)	(.019)		
61	.139**	.019	.037	.634***	.411	.107
	(.071)		(.056)	(.056)		
65	.085	.007	.041**	.961***	.929	.069
	(.071)		(.019)	(.019)		
70	.034	.001	.021	.980***	.960	.053
	(.071)		(.014)	(.014)		
114	.148**	.022	.039*	.942***	.899	.077
	(.071)		(.023)	(.023)		
120	.078	.006	.010	.977	.937	.069
	(.071)		(.018)	(.018)		
150	.132*	.017	.137***	.807***	.669	.082
	(.071)		(.041)	(.041)		
157	.008	.000	−.037	.424	.178	.089
	(.071)		(0.65)	(.065)		
169	.223***	.049	.043***	.958***	.935	.066
	(.070)		(.019)	(.019)		
170	−.114	.013	−.026	.807***	.658	.089
	(.071)		(.042)	(.042)		
178	.200***	.040	.130***	.792***	.663	.123
	(.070)		(.042)	(.042)		
188	.110	.012	−.043	.885***	.773	.096
	(.071)		(.035)	(.035)		
38	.663***	.440	.605***	−.357***	.564	.071
	(.053)		(.048)	(.048)		
56	.072	.005	.184***	.495***	.237	.076
	(.071)		(.064)	(.064)		
67	.198***	.039	.039**	.963***	.941	.051
	(.070)		(.018)	(.018)		
101	.186***	.035	.220***	.794***	.664	.117
	(.070)		(.042)	(.042)		
126	.086	.007	−.079	.774***	.579	.114
	(.071)		(.048)	(.048)		
134	−.036	.01	−.015*	.927***	.862	.106
	(.071)		(.027)	(.027)		
144	.118*	.014	.025	.817***	.672	.092
	(.071)		(.041)	(.041)		

a. Values in columns under each variable name are standardized regression coefficients with their standard errors in parentheses below them.

*Significantly different from zero at the .10 level of significance.

**Significantly different from zero at the .05 level of significance.

***Significantly different from zero at the .01 level of significance.

independent of the generalized agglomerative economies is an important result for industrial location policy. Streit also found the general agglomerative variable to be highly significant for all 52 of his industries, but found the linkage variable to be significant, after removing the effects of G, for 11 industries, five more than for Model 1. Thus, for more highly aggregated data, the addition of the variable, G, may increase the proportion of industries for which the linkage variable is significant, but this is not true for the less highly aggregated industries of this study.

In relating these regression results to the preceding analysis it is notable that the coefficient of the linkage variable is significant for three of the four industries with seven or more links accompanied by geographic associations (see Table 5–8).

The possibility that market orientations rather than general agglomerative economies are a major determinant of associations is tested in Model 3 by including M_{kj} and omitting G_{kj}. Of the varieties of orientation discussed above, market orientation seems to be the one most unequivocally identified. For this reason, Model 3 attempts to control for market orientation by including a measure of it in the equation.

The discussion of the general agglomerative variable above indicated that multiplicative combinations of measures for pairs of industries would be preferred to additive combinations in the regression equation. Thus the measure used in Model 3, M_{kj}, is simply the product of the measures of market orientation for industries k and j. It was expected that the sign of the coefficient for M would be positive reflecting the fact that when the variable has a large value, both industries tend to be market oriented and thus are also geographically associated with each other to the extent that final markets for all industries are population concentrations. The positive value is also expected because market orientation will be credited for explaining some variation due to the omitted variable, G. Usable regression results were obtained for only 13 of the sample industries and are reported in Table 5–10. All 13 coefficients for M are positive and significant (most at the .01 level of significance). Thus market orientation as measured in this study does does seem to be important in explaining variations in the degree of geographic association between industries. The overall results are similar to those for Model 1, however. The values of R^2 are generally low, though not as low as for Model 1, and the standard errors of estimate (not reported) are again high, indicating that the two variables M_{kj} and G_{kj} do not attempt to explain the same variation. The linkage variable L was found to be significantly different from zero for six industries for which this was also true with Model 1 and for one additional industry. The addition of the market orientation variable does seem to improve the explanatory power of the model, but not to the same extent that addition of the general ag-

Table 5–10. Regression results for model 3[a].

Industry	L	M	R²	Industry	L	M	R²
6	−.094	.296***	.085	150	.141**	.145**	.038
	(.070)	(.070)			(.070)	(.070)	
47	.206***	.289***	.144	157	.022	.186***	.035
	(.067)	(.067)			(.071)	(.071)	
61	.135*	.127*	.035	169	.225***	.359***	.178
	(.070)	(.070)			(.065)	(.065)	
65	.104	.257***	.073	170	−.109	.242*	.072
	(.069)	(.069)			(.069)	(.069)	
70	−.000	.336***	.113	178	.230***	.411***	.208
	(.068)	(.068)			(.064)	(.064)	
114	.145**	.233***	.076	188	.129*	.233***	.066
	(.068)	(.068)			(.069)	(.069)	
120	.039	.317***	.112				
	(.068)	(.068)					

a. Values in columns under each variable name are standardized regression coefficients with their standard errors in parentheses below them.
*Significantly different from zero at the .10 level of significance.
**Significantly different from zero at the .05 level of significance.
***Significantly different from zero at the .01 level of significance.

glomerative economy variable does. Thus it is tentatively concluded that both variables should be included in the model.

In model 4, variables were considered for addition to the regression equation to attempt to control for the effects of all the orientations discussed in this study. The general agglomerative variable, G_{kj}, was also included again as in Model 2. Market orientation, M_{kj}, was included as in Model 3. A variable to represent labor orientation, W_{kj}, was formed as the product of the measures of labor orientation for the two industries as described in Chapter 3.[5] Even though the results of the test for nonrandomness in Chapter 3 did not permit identification of footloose industries, a variable representing this factor was formed as the product of the measure of nonrandomness for each of the industries and added to the regression model as N_{kj}.

A variable to represent material orientation for each industry was formed by subtracting from its purchases from primary resource extractors (RESORZ), 7.5% of its total purchases of inputs (INPUTS). As explained in Chapter 3, if the result is positive then the industry is potentially material oriented. To adjust for the degree of realization of the potential, which is measured by a low value for the correlation between industry employment and total population (LOCPOP), the difference, RESORZ − .075 INPUTS, is divided by this correlation. Thus the measure of material orientation is (RESORZ − .075 INPUTS)/LOCPOP. High correlations reduce the size of the measure and low correlations increase it as desired. The variable used to represent material orientation for two industries in the regression model, R_{kj}, is then the product of the measures of material orientation for the two industries.[6]

The results of estimating this model for each industry were high values of R^2 but few significant coefficients. For this reason a stepwise procedure was used with the six variables as candidates for inclusion in the equation for each industry. Table 5–11 reports for each industry the values of the step in which the last statistically significant variable was added.[7] The number of industries for which the measure of potential agglomerative economies, L, is significant rises to 12 from the previous high of 10 in Models 1 and 2. The coefficient of the market orientation variable is significantly different from zero for eight industries, but is negative for three industries indicating that these three industries have fewer associations with industries that are more market oriented once variations in general agglomerative factors and, in one case, labor orientation have been taken into account. The general agglomerative variable, G, is still highly significant for all 20 industries. The coefficient of the material orientation variable is significantly different from zero for only two industries. Neither of these was an indstry with a significant coefficient for market orientation, perhaps indicating that, as one would expect, market and material orientations really are polar cases. The coefficient of the labor orientation variable is significantly different from zero for five industries; it is positive twice and negative three times. One might explain a tendency to reduce the degree of geographic association when both industries are highly labor oriented by noting that two labor oriented industries will not be attracted to the same sites if one requires a distinctive type of labour found in a few areas that have only this kind of labor. The nonrandomness variable has a coefficient significantly different from zero for only two industries, 65 (Paints and Allied Products) and 169 (Electronic Components). In both cases the sign is negative, perhaps reflecting that the less random the locational pattern of an industry. the less likely that its pattern will correspond closely to those of other industries. As in Model 2, the R^2 values are generally high because of the contribution of G and the standard errors of estimate are generally low. Basically, this model shows expected results for the various orientation variables.

While the distinction between demand and supply links was shown not to be useful with different methods in a preceding section, the lack of precise agreement between results reported above and those using regression analysis justifies additional investigation of demand and supply linkages. In order to do this, the linkage variable used in Models 1 to 4, L_{kj}, was separated into supply and demand components, S_{kj} and D_{kj}, as follows:

$$S_{kj} = 1/4 \ (Y_{kj}/I_j + Y_{jk}/I_k)$$
$$D_{kj} = 1/4 \ (Y_{kj}/O_k + Y_{jk}/O_j)$$

Table 5–11. Regression results for model 4 [a].

Industry	L	G	M	R	W	N	Standard error of estimate	R²
6		.965*** (.020)				-.042** (.020)	.063	.924
47		.954*** (.019)	.048*** (.019)				.066	.939
61		.640*** (.055)					.107	.410
65	.038** (.019)	.974*** (.020)	-.057*** (.020)		-.044*** (.019)		.068	.933
70	.024* (.014)	.968*** (.015)	.041*** (.015)				.052	.962
114	.038* (.023)	.959*** (.024)	-.054*** (.024)				.077	.901
120		.958*** (.019)	.033* (.019)				.069	.937
150	.131*** (.041)	.839*** (.043)	-.106*** (.042)				.081	.679
157		.421*** (.065)					.089	.177
169	.075*** (.019)	.933*** (.019)	.077*** (.018)			-.041** (.019)	.062	.943
170		.810*** (.042)					.089	.656

178	.148*** (.040)	.737*** (.042)	.209*** (.043)		.086** (.041)	.117	.699
188		.878*** (.034)				.096	.773
38[b]	.538*** (.055)	−.377*** (.048)		.128*** (.055)		.071	.576
56	.133** (.068)	.494*** (.064)		.111* (.067)		.075	.263
67	.039** (.018)	.963*** (.018)			.108* (.063)	.051	.941
101	.220*** (.042)	.794*** (.042)				.117	.664
126		.746*** (.047)			−.097** (.047)	.113	.582
134	−.051* (.027)	.927*** (.027)				.106	.862
144		.812*** (.041)			−.068* (.041)	.092	.676

a. Values in columns under each variable name are standardized regression coefficients with their standard errors in parentheses below them.

b. M was inadvertently omitted from the stepwise procedure for the last seven industries.

* Significantly different from zero at the .10 level of significance.

** Significantly different from zero at the .05 level of significance.

*** Significantly different from zero at the .01 level of significance.

where O_k and I_k represent total intermediate output and total intermediate input of industry k and Y_{kj} is the value of sales for industry k to industry j. Model 5 is then the same as Model 4 with the linkage variable separated. Again the stepwise procedure was used. The results were very similar to those of Model 4 and for this reason are not reported. In six cases either the demand link or the supply link was significant where L had been in Model 4. In four more cases both D and S had significant coefficients. In two of these four cases the two variables are highly collinear, however, and for this reason use of the L variable might be preferable. For one industry, for which L had been just significant in Model 4, neither D nor S was significant in Model 5, and for one industry, for which L was not significant in Model 4, D was significant in Model 5. The conclusion is that, for some individual industries, it is important to distinguish between demand and supply links.

The results of applying multiple regression techniques to the analysis of variations in geographic associations for individual industries show clearly that different variables are important for different industries. It is also clear that generalized agglomerative factors, as measured here, provide the most significant contribution to explaining geographic associations for single industries. Market orientation was found to be the second most important explanatory variable for more industries than any other factor. The contribution to explaining geographic associations of the potential agglomerative economies represented by a measure of industrial linkages was not as large as had been anticipated, neither in their aggregate form nor when separated into demand and supply linkage measures. However, in this section as in the preceding one a definite positive effect of agglomerative economies arising from transportation cost reductions was found to exist. The next section will consider the extent to which these economies may influence geographic associations of more than two industries.

INDUSTRIAL COMPLEXES

In this section the extension of the analysis of bilateral relationships between one industry and others to the case of industrial complexes is considered. The following paragraphs will show how the information on bilateral relationships developed in preceding sections can be used to identify a kind of industrial complex. The method relies specifically on knowledge of the linkages accompanied by associations for each industry.

Isard defined an industrial complex as a set of activities occurring at a given location, the set being subject to important production, marketing and other interrelationships [22: 375–412]. His approach relied not only on input-output relationships, but also on detailed production, transportation and marketing information. His objective was to analyze hypothetical complexes as part of an attempt to find optimal locations for specific industries or to find viable complexes of industries for specific locations. Both the data requirements and the objectives of Isard's methods make them inappropriate for this study.

Klaassen suggested calculating coefficients of attraction, which calculations require knowledge of both transport costs and regional input-output relationships to determine the demand or supply orientation of industries [25]. This information could be used in determining which industries may form complexes, but the data requirements are too excessive to consider implementation of Klaassen's analysis for the present study.

In the present study an industrial complex is defined as a set of industrial activities, frequently occurring in geographic association with each other, that have important trading links. In Chapter 4 the possibility of using higher order correlation coefficients to discover significant geographic associations of more than two industries was mentioned but not implemented because of computational problems. To identify a complex in the present study an industry is selected from those identified above as having their locations determined in part by linkages. The industries to which it has both significant linkages and associations are listed. When both exist, this will be termed a relationship. The industries which have relationships with those in the first list are then listed. This process is continued for several iterations until circularity occurs or is found to be absent. (Circularity occurs when an industry of a lower numbered iteration reappears at a higher number iteration.) The type of complex identified by this method is likely to be more interdependent than hierarchal in nature as Streit has pointed out [47: 182]. It may be more important to identify this type of complex than a more hierarchal type because the latter type is more readily identifiable simply using associations and the input-output table.[8]

Industry 169, Electronic Components, offers a possible starting point for identifying a complex using the method described. From Table 5–8 we see that it has seven links accompanied by associations and according to Table 5–11 linkages are significant in attempting to explain its geographic associations. As shown in Table 5–12 industry 169 was found to have relationships with industries 148, 164 and 167 which also have relationships with it. Neither industry 148 nor industry 164 possesses any additional reciprocal relationships with industries other than 167 and 169. Industry 167 has such reciprocal relationships with industries 120 and 187. Industry 187 has no other reciprocal relationships but industry 120 has such relationships with industries 45, 47 and 48. The latter three, in turn, have reciprocal relationships with other industries as indicated in Figure 5–1. The figure shows the complex identified by the relationships in Table 5–12. This complex is self-contained, or closed, because there are no industries omitted which have

Table 5–12. *Identification of an industrial complex.*

Industry Number	Has relationship with industries	Which have relationships with industries
169	120	45, 47, 48, 167
	148	167, 169
	164	169
	167	112, 120, 148, 169, 181, 187, 188
	187	50, 167 .
	191	64
	194	
167	112	
	120	45, 47, 48, 167
	148	167, 169
	169	120, 148, 164, 167, 187, 191, 194
	181	169, 178
	187	50, 167
	188	192

reciprocal relationships with those shown.[9] There are other industries which have relationships with those shown in the complex, but none of those shown has a reciprocal relationship with any industry not in the complex. Thus, mutual interdependence is stressed in this formulation.

In Figure 5–1 an arrow from one industry to another indicates a relationship from the first to the second. Arrows in both directions indicate a reciprocal relationship. Numbers in parentheses are coefficients of correlation measuring geographic associations and the letters D, S, SD and SS refer, respectively, to demand, supply, strong demand and strong supply links from the initial to the terminal industry of the nearest arrow. Clearly, industries 148, 167 and 169 are part of an industrial complex because each has strong relationships with the other two. Industries 164 and 187 are probably additional members of the complex. Industry 120 might also be included in the complex or it could be considered to be the key industry in a small complex formed by industries 47, 48 and 120. Along with industry 45, industry 120 could also be considered to be part of the complex formed by industries 50, 51, 53 and 47. However, the industries in Figure 5–1 are ultimately divided into complexes, the central roles played by industries 167, 120 and 51 are clear.[10]

The linkage information in Figure 5–1 can be used to comment further on some of the interdependencies that have been accompanied by geographic associations among these industries. In most cases where a reciprocal relationship exists, one industry is more strongly linked to the other. For example, the electronic components industry (169) is strongly linked in demand and supply to the electric instruments industry (148) as is the communication equipment industry (167). The electric instruments industry (148) has only weak links to each of these, however,

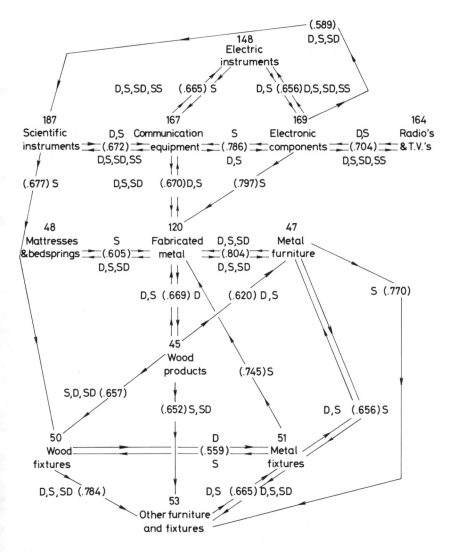

Fig. 5–1. Identification of Industrial Complexes. Numbers above abbreviated industry names are industry numbers. Numbers in parentheses are coefficients of geographic associa- tion. D, S, SD and SS represent demand, supply, strong demand and strong supply links from initial industry to terminal industry on nearest arrow.

and might be considered less dependent on them than they are on it. The existence of both demand and supply links from one member of a pair to the other in many cases may indicate that even within the four-digit SIC industries used here there are quite different firms.

The method of identifying a complex used here is similar to that used by

Streit [47: 182]. According to Streit's method, a complex exists only if for all pairs of industries in the complex both 1. the coefficient of correlation measuring geographic association is statistically greater than zero (at some level of significance), and 2. the average value of the four linkage relationships between the pair is greater than the average value of this average for at least one member of the pair. All significant measures of association in the present study have values greater than .5 at the .05 level of significance, so that Streit's criterion 1. is fulfilled for all pairs in a complex identified by the methods of the present study. The average value of the average of the four possible links between one industry and another was computed for industries 47,120 and 169. Table 5–13 shows these values and the values of the average linkage with a number of other industries from Figure 5–1. The table shows that the method used in identifying a complex illustrated above results in Streit's second criterion being fulfilled for 13 of 15 pairs. Thus while Streit's criterion is less stringent than that used here for geographic associations, and his criterion for linkages is slightly more stringent the complexes indentified using the two methods would probably be quite similar. Detailed comparisons with complexes identified by Streit are not possible because of the level of aggregation in his study.

Czamanski used a potentially powerful method for identifying industrial complexes which is essentially an application factor analysis (1).[11] The

Table 5–13. Comparison of industry average and single pair links.

Industry (i)	$\dfrac{\sum\limits_{j=1}^{n} L_{ij}}{n}$	Linked and associated industries (j)	L_{ij}
47	.00472	45	.00659
		51	.02416
		53	.01610
		120	.02488
120	.00483	45	.00922
		51	.00942
		47	.02488
		48	.03741
		167	.01402
		169	.00244*
169	.00882	120	.00244*
		148	.05969
		164	.12524
		167	.17883
		187	.01369

*Indicates average link between industry *i* and industry *j* is less than average of all links for industry *i*.

factors are complexes and are derived from a matrix of measures of similarity in trading patterns for individual industries. The method is described in more detail in Appendix Section B–2. It is superior to the method used in this study and to Streit's in that the complexes may contain industries that do not trade with each other at all but which have similar trading patterns with other industries. However, both methods discussed above are superior to Czamanski's in requiring that the potential complexes identified from linkages be shown to have been realized in geographic associations before a complex is identified.

As mentioned in Chapter 3, Czamanski's method of identifying supply linkages is somewhat questionable so that an application of his technique in detail would be inappropriate. Application of his general technique with appropriate modifications was not feasible for the present study because it would have required the calculation of approximately 160,000 more correlation coefficients than were otherwise required. Czamanski's applications of the technique were to too highly aggregated industries to permit detailed comparisons.

This section has shown that the measures of geographic association and potential agglomerative economies arising from transportation cost reductions employed in this study can be used to identify a type of industrial complex that is characterized by a high degree of mutual interdependence. The method has also been compared favorably with other methods of identifying industrial complexes.

SUMMARY

This chapter has analyzed some of the effects of potential agglomerative economies arising from transportation cost reductions and measured by industrial linkages, and other factors on geographic associations of industries. This was done first by considering the aggregate nature of orientation, linkage and association findings for individual industries and then by applying regression analysis to data for single industries. With the first sort of analysis, distinctions between the effects of supply and demand and weak and strong linkages were found not to be significant in the aggregate. Systematic variation, as expected, in aggregate association behavior was found to exist among industry orientation categories. The basic conclusion for aggregate manufacturing industry was that the effects of agglomerative economies on geographic association were small but significant.

Regression analysis of five models for a sample of 20 industries revealed considerable variation in the determinants of geographic association behavior by industry without any strong systematic relations to orientation categories. Agglomerative economies arising from transportation cost reductions, however, were found to be an important explanatory variable for a number of the sample industries, and general agglomerative economies were found to be highly significant for all industries in the sample. The distinction between supply and demand linkages was also found to be significant for some industries.

The last section showed how the measures developed previously can be used to identify a kind of industrial complex illustrating a high degree of interdependence among the component industries. Chapter 6 will summarize the results of the entire study, discuss the policy conclusions that seem justified on the basis of the study and suggest ways of extending and improving the analysis.

NOTES

1. All three of these values are significantly greater than 0 at the .01 level of significance and significantly different from each other at the .01 level. Streit thought that the value of .13 was not statistically significant, and so stated. He apparently used the number of industries rather than the number of different industry pairs as the sample size in computing his test statistics [47: 179].

2. Another way of analyzing the importance of processing stage for individual industries is to consider the relative importance of input sources and output purchases for the average industry. The average number of input source industries for the 199 manufacturing industries in this study is 94.77 and the average number of industries purchasing an industry's output is 69.52. This large difference alone suggests that any single output purchaser might be potentially more important locationally than any single input source to an industry. Table 5-4 shows that there are significantly more (at the .05 level) supply links than demand links per industry, however, indicating that more input sources are important to the average industry. This is because the ratio of number of supply links to number of input sources is not significantly different from the ratio of number of demand links to number of output purchasers so that the larger number of input sources is transformed into a large number of supply links. The only factor supporting the importance of output purchasers is that the number of strong demand links is significantly larger than the number of strong supply links.

3. Klaassen [25b] and Spiegelman [44] also employed regression analysis in their studies of locational behavior but their objectives and approaches were somewhat different and thus their results are not strictly comparable to those of the present study. While the objective of the present study is explicitly to explain geographic associations, Spiegelman's was to explain the level of output using characteristics of the region and Klaassen's was to explain the level of output using characteristics of the industry, including its supply and demand relationships with other industries. Use of these relationships makes Klaassen's analysis more closely related to that of this study. It is interesting that he, too, finds that interindustry links are important locational variables. Because he examined only three-digit SIC industries for larger regions, direct comparisons of the magnitude of effects is not possible.

4. Note that only seven of the ten industries are the same in both cases. For industry 134 the sign of L is negative but, because the value of the coefficient is not significantly less than zero at the .05 level of significance and because the theoretical model cannot explain a negative influence of a linkage, it might be regarded as zero.

5. In the actual calculating of the regression equations the reciprocal of the measure described in Chapter 3 was used.

6. While the general agglomeration variable is related to the measures of market and

material orientation used in this study these variables are not highly colinear. G is based on the correlation between regional employment for a specific industry and total regional employment while M and R utilize the correlation between regional employment in an industry and total regional population. Total regional population is highly correlated with total regional employment. G is not highly correlated with M or R, however, because the latter two variables use additional information that is not correlated with total regional employment.

7. The inclusion of only variables with coefficients significantly different from zero means that the estimated equations for industries 67, 101 and 134 are identical to those reported in Table 5–9 for Model 2.

8. Leontieff has suggested a means of identifying the hierarchal structure of industry by 'triangulation' of an input-output table [27: 4]. In this process, material oriented industries are listed first, then the industries linked to them, and so on until the market oriented industries might be omitted from the complex. Links to industries in the study but not in with specifying industry orientations uniquely.

9. This statement applies to the 199 industries used in the study. Reciprocal relationships with industries not in the study might exist; but the only error possible is that some industries might be omitted from the complex. Links to industries in the study but not in the complex could be important for some not shown. However, it remains true that among those industries in the complex, each might be interested in the location of another in it which might reciprocate this interest. For example, a firm producing electric instruments would be interested in being close to a firm producing electronic components and the latter would like to locate close to the former. The presence of both of these would make a location highly attractive to a firm producing communications equipment.

10. Note that other practitioners have allowed the same industry to be part of more than one complex so that it is not necessary to allocate each industry to only one complex.

11. Stevens, Douglas and Neighbor report that they attempted a factor analysis approach to the identification of complexes several years prior to 1969. Unfortunately they do not specify what the results of the attempt were [46: 21].

6. Summary of results and conclusions

This chapter first summarizes the findings of the investigation described in the preceding chapters. The implications that these findings have for the kinds of policy questions posed in Chapter 1 are then briefly commented upon. Ways in which this investigation might be improved and extended are then discussed.

SUMMARY OF PRECEDING CHAPTERS

In Chapter 1 the study of industrial location was justified and a model of industrial location was presented. It specified that the locations of firms in manufacturing industries would be determined by the degree to which they respond to low-cost labor markets, sources of raw materials used, sites of final consumers of their products, and locations of other manufacturing industries. The force motivating a locational response to any of these factors would be the desire to maximize profits by reducing transportation costs. In Chapter 5 an additional factor representing the cost reductions available to firms simply by locating in a large industrial center, regardless of the particular industries present, and not arising from transportation costs, was added to the model. The extent to which firms may have reduced transportation costs by locating near other manufacturing industries with which they trade was identified as the primary objective of the investigation.

Chapter 2 discussed in considerable detail the data that were used in the study. A set of 377 regions completely spanning the U.S. and considering metropolitan and nonmetropolitan areas separately was developed. The method of estimating employment in 199 four-digit SIC industries for the 377 regions was described. Examination of the employment estimates revealed them to be at least acceptable if not good. The source of data on trading relationships among industries, an input-output study, was also discussed.

In Chapter 3 measures of factors influencing location were developed after first concluding that industry in the U.S. does not locate randomly according to one weak test. Potential labor orientation of firms was measured by the relative cost of wages in the firm's processing costs (the ratio of wages to value added was used as a proxy for this), and 51 industries were identified as being potentially labor oriented. Probable orientation to final consumer markets was identified for 36 industries which sold a significant proportion of their output to the final demand sector and which also tended to locate close to consumer markets (measured by population concentrations). Probable orientation toward primary resource extractors was identified for 28 industries which purchased a significant proportion of their output from the primary resource sectors and which also tended not to locate near to population concentrations (assuming that primary resource locations do not correspond to those of population concentrations). A means of identifying potential orientation toward other manufacturing firms because of possible reductions in transportation costs on traded products using industrial linkages was then discussed in comparison with previous measures. A large number of potential agglomerative economies falling into supply-demand and weak-strong categories was found to exist among the industries of the study.

Chapter 4 explored measures of the degree to which firms in different industries tend to locate close to each other. The coefficient of correlation between regional employment estimates for pairs of industries was justified as the most suitable measure. A significant locational association was found to exist between more than 5% of all industry pairs. Variation in the measure between metropolitan and nonmetropolitan regions suggested that only by including all geographic areas would truly general locational characteristics of industries be identified. Variation in the measure of geographic association with size of industry cluster was found to be inconsistent except that the largest clusters were identified as producing the most significant associations. Geographic associations among firms in more than two industries were not examined because the volume of calculations required for such an examination with available methods was felt to be excessive.

In Chapter 5 the impact of the measure of potential agglomerative economies arising from transportation cost reductions on the measure of geographic association for 199 manufacturing industries in the aggregate was first discussed. A small but measurable positive influence was found. The aggregate influence did not seem to be affected substantially by separate consideration of linkages to suppliers and consumers or of weak and strong links as defined in Chapter 3. The response of firms ir the aggregate did seem to be affected by their identification as market or material oriented according to the methods of Chapter 3. Regression analysis of a sample of 20 individual industries revealed that agglomerative ecoromies based on transportation cost reductions were important in determining geographic associations for more than half of the sample industries. General agglomerative economies were even more important; they were significant for all of the sample industries. Each of the other location factors was found to have a significant impact on the geographic associations of at least two industries, but only market orientation had a substantial effect. Finally, the bilateral relationships developed earlier were used to identify an industrial complex characterized by a high degree of mutual interdependence.

IMPLICATIONS FOR INDUSTRIAL LOCATION PRACTICE AND POLICY

The literature on public policies intended to influence industrial location decisions of firms is extensive. Most writers recognize that in all economies which allow firms to make their own location decisions, firms can be assumed to choose locations which maximize returns to the decision makers.[1] Therefore public policies, if they are to have any effect, must have an impact on the rates of return possible at specific sites. In his 1948 book, Hoover [18: 251–278] outlined the major kinds of policies that can be used. As he shows, public agencies have within their control a variety of means of affecting returns, primarily through the firm's costs. The major categories include those affecting 1. the labor market (through standards, wage subsidies, training programs, information services and mobility policies); 2. the capital market (through low interest loans, loan guarantees, and investment credits); 3. the land market (through zoning and other restriction, land assembly for industrial parks and the development and pricing of utilities); 4. the transportation market (through the location and type of facilities constructed and the prices for use established); and 5. taxes, which may affect any of the other markets. Klaassen [25a] has surveyed some ways in which the various types of policies have been employed.

Because public agencies in free economies affect industrial location only through firms' costs, it is not necessary to recognize public activity as a distinct factor of location. In fact a kind of opposite is true: public agencies need to recognize the strengths of the locational orientations of firms in various industries, which are based on costs, if they are to successfully pursue industrial location programs, especially when such programs have as their goal the attraction of new industries and when the means available to implement the programs are only taxes and subsidies. Certainly funds should not be wasted attempting to attract to nonmetropolitan regions firms in industries identified as being highly responsive to markets and general agglomerative factors. Empirical findings confirm that 'more basic, economic factors still determine the choice of region of location, and that tax and subsidy policies . . . are not important in and of themselves' [45: 11]. These policies are marginal in influencing industrial location but, in the short run, they may be all that is available to a regional development agency. If tax and subsidy policies are to be used effectively the regional development agency must have an understanding of the basic economic factors influencing location. This study has outlined a methodology and has also produced some results that might contribute significantly to such an understanding. Given the normally limited resources (in the form of tax concessions and subsidies, as well as funds for promoting development) of regional development agencies, they should attempt to use these as efficiently as possible. One possible way of improving the efficiency of such agencies might be for them to concentrate their efforts on attracting firms in industries which are not oriented to factors not present in the region and which are frequently both geographically associated and linked, through potential agglomerative economies arising from transportation cost reductions with firms already in the region.[2] In this case the development agency would be attempting to reduce other costs just enough so that the potential transportation cost reduction would become the dominant consideration in a firm's location decision. The existence of the possibility that this might occur for firms in a specific industry could be determined in advance through the methods proposed in this study.

Another approach would be to attempt to induce all of the industries in a small complex to locate in a region. If a new complex is to be attracted, the most resources might be devoted to attracting the key industry in the complex. Another possibility is to operate directly on the size of the potential agglomerative economy. This can be accomplished by reducing substantially intraregional transfer costs. These can be reduced by insuring that all industries can be located together, as in well-designed industrial parks. Transfer costs can also be reduced by providing improved intra-regional transportation facilities such as the 'ring' type of superhighways which have been constructed around many cities in the U.S. (Boston even has two rings at different distances from the central city.)

The extended complex, or set of interrelated complexes appearing in Figure 5–1 above illustrates another important point: formal analysis of the type proposed in this study may identify industries that might have been ignored as potential candidates for attraction without the analysis. A priori, one might not consider electric instruments and furniture of any kind to be related as closely as they seem to be.

From the viewpoint of individual firms, one might be more doubtful of the usefulness of the kind of analysis discussed in this study. However, it could be important for a firm to know where all the other firms in its industry have located and with which industries they have usually been associated (this might reveal previously unknown reasons for some firms being more successful than others). Knowledge of the geographic distribution and locational factors of a firm's markets and suppliers could also be valuable.

The potential utility of this kind of study has only been suggested in the preceding paragraphs; other implications and applications are possible. The value of this kind of study both to the theory of industrial location and in the area of industrial location policy and practice might be increased in ways suggested in the following section.

SUGGESTED EXTENSIONS OF THE ANALYSIS

At several points in the preceding chapters limits were imposed on the scope of the investigation. The removal of these might be a useful way of extending the analysis. More confidence might be placed in the findings with respect to the importance of agglomerative economies to manufacturing industry as a whole if all manufacturing industries were included in the investigation. Computational algorithms are available which would permit such an expansion of the number of industries. Statements regarding the importance of various factors for the location of firms in individual industries would be much more valid if regression analysis of all industries instead of only 20 industries had been completed. Conclusions regarding urban-rural differences and the effect of threshold size should also be based on results from all industries instead of small samples.

An important trend in industrial location in recent decades has been the suburbanization of much manufacturing activity. Extension of the examination of urban-rural differences in geographic association to separate treatment of suburban and central city areas of SMSA's might yield new information regarding the forces involved in the suburbanization.

Problems with the attempt to identify footloose industries and a threshold size effect were mentioned in Chapters 3 and 4. These might be overcome through experimentation with different criteria for identifying each. Experimentation with more and less stringent criteria for identifying potentially significant agglomerative economies and for identifying significant geographic associations might produce a combination of criteria to identify positively only those industries subject to a significant impact. Systematic examination of the distributions of these measures for all industries would probably be helpful in this regard. Estimation of more regression models for individual industries, including alternative specifications of functional forms, would probably produce better models.

The analysis of industrial complexes could be improved significantly by combining the use of higher order correlation coefficients to identify geographic associations (as described in Chapter 4) with factor analysis techniques (described in Chapter 5) for identifying similar trading patterns for industries.

The validity of the methods used in this study and suggested in the preceding paragraphs might also be examined. One way of approaching such a validation would be to systematically compare the results of specific regional, industry and firm studies to those of the aggregate industrial approach used here. Hopefully the results would show that individual firms and regions do not differ greatly in characteristics or behavior from industries in the aggregate. More accurate estimates of regional industry employment might also contribute to the analysis.

A final, and potentially the most significant, way in which this investigation might be extended would be to utilize time series observations on both locational and input-output structures. One hypothesis of interest might be that, over time, more significant linkages are accompanied by geographic associations in an industry indicating, among other possibilities, that competitive conditions force firms to take advantage of all possible economies and that the competitive model is still valid for the economy. Rejection of the hypothesis might, instead, be interpreted to mean that reductions in transportation costs have reduced the importance of agglomerative economies.

There are, no doubt, many other ways in which the analysis presented in this study could be extended and improved. The author believes that the methods of the previous chapters themselves represent significant extensions and improvements in comparison to previous work in this area.

NOTES

1. Note that this statement recognizes that managers whose compensation is not clearly tied to firm profits may choose locations that maximize their own satisfaction. It is assumed that such behavior is more significant intraregionally than interregionally.
2. This is essentially the approach advocated by Klaassen when he discusses attraction of 'complementary' industries [25b: 110].

List of references

1. Alexander, John W. and James B. Lindberg, Measurements of Manufacturing: Coefficients of Correlation, *Journal of Regional Science* (April 1963), 71–81.
2. Artle, Roland, *The Structure of the Stockholm Economy*. Cornell University Press, Ithaca, New York 1965.
3. Bain, Joe S., *Barriers to New Competition: Their Character and Consequences in Manufacturing Industries*. Harvard University Press, Cambridge 1966.
4. Bos, H. C., *Spatial Dispersion of Economic Activity*. Rotterdam University Press, Rotterdam 1965.
5. Braschler, Curtis H., Importance of Manufacturing in Area Economic Growth, *Land Economics* (February 1971), 109–111.
6. Cameron, Gordon C., On Attracting Industry to Developing Areas, unpublished paper delivered at Southern Economic Association Meetings, November 8, 1968.
7. Chinitz, Benjamin, Contrasts in Agglomeration: New York and Pittsburg, *American Economic Review* (May 1961), 270–289.
8. Czamanski, S., A Model of Urban Growth *Regional Science Association Papers* (1965), 177–200.
9. *Czamanski, S.*, Some Empirical Evidence of the Strengths of Linkages Between Groups of Related Industries in Urban-Regional Complexes, *Regional Science Association Papers* (1971), 137–150.
10. Difiglio, C. and B. H. Stevens, Size Distribution of Manufacturing Establishments and their Relationships to Employment Size of Industrial Counties, unpublished Regional Science Research Institute discussion paper.
11. Duncan, Otis Dudley *et al.*, *Metropolis and Region*. Resourcs for the Future, Baltimore 1960.
12. Dziewonski, K., A New Approach to Theory and Empirical Analysis of Location, *Regional Science Association Papers* (1966), 17–25.
13. Florence, P. Sargent, *Investment, Location and Size of Plant*. Cambridge University Press, Cambridge 1948.
14. Fuchs, Victor R., *Changes in the Location of Manufacturing in the United States since 1929*. Yale University Press, New Haven and London 1962.
15. Greenhut, Melvin L., *Plant Location in Theory and Practice*. University of North Carolina Press, Chapel Hill 1956.
16. Harris, Chauncy D., The Market as a Factor in the Localization of Industry in the U.S., *Annals of the Association of American Geographers* (December 1954), 315–348.
17. Hoover, Edgar M., *Location Theory and the Shoe and Leather Industries*. Harvard University press, Cambridge 1937.
18. Hoover, Edgar M., *The Location of Economic Activity*. McGraw-Hill Book Co., New York 1948.
19. Hoover, Edgar M., *Trends in Location and Location Theory*. Center for Regional Economic Studies Occasional Paper No. 6. University of Pittsburg, Pittsburg October 1968.
20. *Industrial Development and Manufacturers Record* (October 1969), 79–242, 1969 International Site Selection Handbook.
21. Isard, Walter, *Location and Space Economy*. The M.I.T. Press, Cambridge 1956.
22. Isard, Walter, *Methods of Regional Analysis: An Introduction to Regional Science*. Cambridge: The M.I.T. Press, 1960.
23. Isard, Walter and Thomas W. Langford, *Regional Input-Output Study: Recollections, and Diverse Notes on the Philadelphia Experience*. The M.I.T. Press, Cambridge 1971.

24. Johnston, J., *Econometric Methods*. McGraw-Hill Book Co., New York 1963.
25. Klaassen, Leo H., The Analysis of Industrial Relationships in Location Theory, *Regional Science Association Papers* (1966), 123–128.
25a. Klaassen, Leo H., *Area Economic and Social Redevelopment: Guidelines for Programmes*. Organization for Economic Cooperation and Development, Paris 1965.
25b. Klaassen, Leo H., *Methods of Selecting Industries for Depressed Areas*. Organization for Economic Cooperation and Development, Paris 1968.
26. Kuh, Edwin and John R. Meyer, Correlation and Regression Estimates When the Data Are Ratios, *Econometrica* (October 1955), 400–416.
27. Leontieff, Wassily, The Structure of Development, *Scientific American* (September 1963), 25–35.
28. Leontieff, Wassily, The Structure of the U.S. Economy, *Scientific American* (April 1965), 22–35.
29. Lichtenberg, Robert M., *One-Tenth of a Nation*. Harvard University Press, Cambridge 1960.
30. Longini, Arthur, *Region of Opportunity: Industrial Potential along the Pittsburg-Youngstown Axis*. Pittsburg and Lake Erie Railroad Company, 1961.
31. Lösch, August, *The Economics of Location*. Translated from the Second Revised Edition by William H. Woglom with the Assistance of Wolfgang F. Stolper. John Wiley & Sons, New York 1952.
32. Marcus, Matityahu, Agglomerative Economies: A Suggested Approach, *Land Economics* (August 1965), 279–284.
33. McCamely, Francis, Testing for Spatially Autocorrelated Disturbances with Application to Relationships Estimated Using Missouri County Data, unpublished paper presented at Fourth Annual Meeting of the Mid-Continent Section, Regional Science Association in Bloomington, Indiana, March 31, 1972.
34. McCarty, Harold J., J. C. Hook and D. S. Knos, *The Measurement of Association in Industrial Geography*. State University of Iowa Press, Iowa City 1956.
35. Menchik, Mark D., Testing Theories of Spatial Equilibrium: A New Procedure, *Journal of Regional Science* (August 1971), 153–172.
36. Mishan, E. J., The Postwar Literature on Externalities: An Interpretive Essay, *Journal of Economic Literature* (March 1971), 1–28.
37. Morrison, Joel L., Morton W. Scripter and Robert H. T. Smith, Basic Measures of Manufacturing in the United States, 1958, *Economic Geography* (October 1968), 296–311.
38. Perloff, Harvey S. *et al.*, *Regions, Resources and Economic Growth*. Resources for the Future, Baltimore 1960.
39. Pred, Allan, The Concentration of High-Value-Added Manufacturing, *Economic Geography* (January 1965), 108–132.
40. Richardson, Harry W., *Elements of Regional Economics*. Penguin Books, Baltimore 1969.
41. Richter, Charles Edward, *The Impact of Industrial Linkages on Geographic Association*. Unpublished Ph.D. Dissertation, University of Illinois, 1968.
42. Richter, Charles Edward, The Impact of Industrial Linkages on Geographic Association, *Journal of Regional Science*, 9 (1969), 19–28.
43. Smith, Wilfred, *Geography and the Location of Industry*. Liverpool University Press, Liverpool 1952.
44. Spiegelman, Robert G., *A Study of Industry Location Using Multiple Regression Techniques*. Agricultural Economic Report No. 10. Economic Research Service, Department of Agriculture, Washington, D.C. 1968.
45. Stevens, Benjamin H. and Carolyn A. Brackett, *Industrial Location: A Review and Annotated Bibliography of Theoretical, Empirical and Case Studies*. Regional Science Research Institute, Philadelphia 1967.
46. Stevens, Benjamin H., Robert C. Douglas and Carolyn B. Neighbor, *Trends in Industrial Location and Their Impact on Regional Economic Development*. Regional Science Research Institute Discussion Paper No. 31. Regional Science Research Institute, Philadelphia 1969.
47. Streit, M. E., Spatial Associations and Economic Linkages between Industries, *Journal of Regional Science* (August 1969), 177–188.

48. Takayama, T. and G. G. Judge, Equilibrium among Spatially Separated Markets: A Reformulation, *Econometrica* (October 1964), 510–524.
49. Tiebout, Charles M., Location Theory, Empirical Evidence, and Economic Evolution, *Papers of the Regional Science Association* (1957), 74–86.
50. U.S. Department of Commerce. Bureau of the Census, *County and City Data Book, 1967*.
51. Herhalen. *1963 Census of Manufactures, Location of Manufacturing Plants by County, Industry, and Employment Size*.
52. Herhalen. *1963 Census of Manufacturers*, Vol. II, *Industry Statistics*.
53. Herhalen. *1963 Census of Manufacturers*, Vol. III, *Area Statistics*.
54. U.S. Department of Commerce. Business and Defense Services Administration. *Industry Profiles 1958–1967*.
55. U.S. Department of Commerce. Economic Development Administration. *How to Improve Your Community by Attracting New Industry* (March 1970).
56. U.S. Department of Commerce. Office of Business Economics. *Input-Output Structure of the U.S. Economy, 1963*, Vol. I, *Transactions Data for Detailed Industries* (A supplement to the *Survey of Current Business*).
57. Weber, Alfred, *Theory of the Location of Industries*. Translated with an Introduction and Notes by Carl J. Friedrich. University of Chicago Press, Chicago 1929.
58. Worcester, Dean A. Jr. Pecuniary and Technological Externalities, Factor Rents and Social Costs, *American Economic Review* (December 1969), 873–885.
59. Yamane, Taro, *Statistics, An Introductory Analysis*. Harper & Row, New York 1967.

Appendix A

Section A–1

SUBSTITUTION OF SEA'S FOR SMSA'S IN THE NORTHEAST

Twenty-three SMSA's in the Northeast include only parts of counties. Because 4-digit SIC industry data are available only on a whole county basis, these 23 SMSA's were omitted from the SMSA's used in the present study, leaving a total of 193 SMSA's to be included. Of the 27 counties included in the 23 omitted SMSA's, 18 are included in 12 New England Metropolitan State Economic Areas (SEA's). These 12 SEA's are used as being equivalent to SMSA's as regions in the present study, making the total number of regions 377. The nine remaining counties of the excluded SMSA's are included in non-SMSA regions. Two of these might have been included as SMSA's (Androscogin, Maine and New London, Connecticut) but were not for reasons of consistency of treatment.

Tables A–1, A–2 and A–3 list the omitted SMSA's, the included SEA's,

Table A–1. List of 23 omitted SMSA'S.

SMSA and component counties	Number of SEA* of which county is a part	Population in SMSA (1960)	Total county population (1960)
1. Boston, Mass.	–	2,595,481	–
Essex	1	308,057	568,831
Middlesex	1	975,287	1,238,742
Plymouth	3	74,290	248,449
Norfolk	1	446,524	510,526
Suffolk	1	791,329	791,329
2. Bridgeport, Conn.	–	337,983	–
Fairfield	2	296,321	643,589
New Haven	7	41,662	660,315
3. Brockton, Mass.	–	149,458	–
Bristol	4	9,078	398,488
Norfolk	1	20,629	510,256
Plymouth	3	119,751	248,449
4. Fall River, Mass. – R.I.	–	138,156	–
Bristol, Mass.	4	128,695	398,488
Newport, R.I.	–	9,461	81,891
5. Fitchburg-Leominster, Mass.	–	90,158	–
Middlesex	1	8,852	1,238,742
Worcester	12	81,306	583,228

SMSA and component counties	Number of SEA* of which county is a part	Population in SMSA (1960)	Total county population (1960)
6. Hartford, Conn.	–	549,249	–
Hartford	5	508,868	689,555
Middlesex	–	6,780	88,865
Tolland	–	33,601	68,737
7. Lawrence-Haverhill, Mass. – N.H.	–	199,136	–
Essex, Mass.	1	185,592	568,831
Rockingham, N.H.	–	13,544	99,029
8. Lewiston-Auburn, Me.	–	70,295	–
Androscoggin	–	70,295	83,312
9. Lowell, Mass.	–	164,243	–
Middlesex	1	164,243	
10. Manchester, N.H.	–	102,861	–
Hillsborough	6	99,148	178,161
Merrimack	–	3,713	67,785
11. Meriden, Conn.	–	51,850	–
New Haven	7	51,859	660,315
12. New Bedford, Mass.	–	143,176	–
Bristol	4	137,178	398,488
Plymouth	3	5,998	248,449
13. New Britain, Conn.	–	129,397	–
Harford	5	129,397	689,555
14. New Haven, Conn.	–	320,836	–
New Haven	7	320,836	660,315
15. New London-Groton-Norwich, Conn.,	–	170,981	–
New London	–	170,981	185,745
16. Norwalk, Conn.	–	96,756	–
Fairfield	2	96,756	653,589
17. Pittsfield, Mass.	–	76,772	–
Berkshire	8	76,772	142,135
18. Portland, Me.	–	139,122	–
Cumberland	9	139,122	182,751
19. Providence-Pawtucket- Warwick, R.I.-Mass.	–	182,101	–
Bristol, R.I.	10	37,146	37,146
Kent, R.I.	10	111,150	112,619
Newport, R.I.	–	2,267	81,891
Providence, R.I.	10	558,074	568,778
Washington, R.I.	–	22,421	59,054
Bristol, Mass.	4	55,247	398,488
Norfolk, Mass.	1	27,799	510,256
Worcester, Mass.	1	6,697	583,228
20. Springfield-Chicopee- Holyoke, Mass.-Conn.	–	493,999	–
Hampden, Mass.	11	422,254	429,353
Hampshire, Mass.	11	64,660	103,229
Worchester, Mass.	12	3,383	583,228
Tolland, Conn.	–	3,702	68,737
21. Stamford, Conn.	1	178,409	–
Fairfield, Conn.	2	178,409	653,589
22. Waterbury, Conn.	–	185,548	–
Litchfield	–	24,597	119,856
New Haven	7	160,951	660,351
23. Worcester, Mass.	–	328,898	–
Worcester	12	328,898	583,228

Table A–2. List of 12 metropolitan state economic areas.

The following example explains the entries in the table. All of SEA 1 (Boston-Lawrence-Haverhill-Lowell, Mass.) essentially replaces SMSA's 1 (Boston, Mass.) 7 (Lawrence-Haverhill, Mass.) and 9 (Lowell, Mass.). All of Essex County, Mass. is included in SEA 1. Parts of it were included in SMSA 1 and SMSA 7. These parts included 86.8% of the 1960 population of Essex County. The remaining 13.2% (100%–86.8%) of the population that was not previously included in any SMSA is now included in SEA 1. All of Norfolk County is also included in SEA 1. Parts of Norfolk County were included in SMSA's 1, 3 and 19.3.1% (100–96.9%) of Norfolk County's population that was included in no SMSA is included in SEA 1.

SEA and component counties	SMSA numbers* of which county was a part	% of total county population included in all SMSA's
1. Boston-Lawrence-Haverhill-Lowell, Mass.		
Essex	1, 7	86.8
Middlesex	1, 5, 9	92.7
Norfolk	1, 3, 19	96.9
Suffolk	–	100.0
2. Bridgeport-Stamford-Norwalk, Conn.		
Fairfield	2, 16, 21	87.4
3. Brockton, Mass.		
Plymouth	1, 3, 12	80.5
4. Fall River-New Bedford, Mass.		
Bristol	3, 4, 12, 19	82.9
5. Hartford-New Britain, Conn.		
Hartford	6, 13	92.3
6. Manchester, N.H.		
Hillsborough	10	55.7
7. New Haven-Waterbury-Meriden, Conn.		
New Haven	2, 11, 14, 22	87.1
8. Pittsfield, Mass.		
Berkshire	17	54.0
9. Portland, Me.		
Cumberland	18	76.1
10. Providence-Pawtucket-Warwick, R.I.		
Bristol	19	100.0
Kent	19	98.7
Providence	19	98.1
11. Springfield-Chicopee-Holyoke, Mass.		
Hampden	20	98.3
Hampshire	20	62.3
12. Worcester-Fitchburg-Leominster, Mass.		
Worcester	5, 19, 20, 23	72.0

*SMSA numbers are those used in Table A–1.

*Table A–3. List of SMSA counties omitted from SEA's but
included in non-SMSA OBE regions.*

The nine counties below were partially included in some of
the 23 omitted SMSA's. They are omitted from the 12 SEA's
but included in the non-SMSA OBE regions indicated.

County	SMSA's (from Table A–1) which contain part of the county	% of the 1960 population of the county in all SMSA's	Number of region in which all of county is included
1. Litchfield County, Conn.	22	20.5	210
2. Middlesex County, Conn.	6	7.6	210
3. New London County, Conn.	15	92.1	210
4. Tolland County, Conn.	6, 20	54.3	210
5. Androscoggin County, Me.	8	81.4	207
6. Merrimack County, N.H.	10	5.5	208
7. Rockingham County, N.H.	7	13.7	208
8. Newport County, R.I.	4, 19	14.3	209
9. Washington County, R.I.	19	38.0	209

and the counties in the omitted SMSA's that are not in the included SEA's.
Additional characteristics of these which permit a rough evaluation of the
effects of using the SEA's as if they were actually SMSA's and of placing
certain counties which were partially included in SMSA's in the rest of OBE
regions are also in these tables. Although population is only one of the
characteristics used in defining SMSA's and SEA's, the population characteristics listed in the tables can be interpreted as supporting the procedure
used in this study. The percentage of a county's population included in an
SMSA is generally much higher among the 18 counties included in the 12
SEA's than among the nine SMSA counties omitted from SEA's. (The
average percentage in the first case is 84.5 while in the second it is only 36.4.)

A disadvantage of SEA's in comparison with SMSA's is that they do not
cross state boundaries. However, the use of SEA's in place of SMSA's
seems justified in this study, especially when compared with the alternatives
of 1. omitting a large amount of data from the analysis, 2. using whole
states (as Richter did), or 3. defining some other type of regions based on
counties without the resources to proceed as thoroughly as did the agencies
that defined the SEA's.

Section A–2

METHOD OF SELECTING 199 INDUSTRIES USED

The 1963 Input-Output Study includes approximately 260 manufacturing industries. Fifty-one of these were eliminated from the study because they are not single four-digit industries. After excluding all non-four-digit industries, an additional nine were selected for exclusion by numbering all industries which might potentially be included, and randomly selecting those to be excluded from among these.[1]

The industries included seem to provide a good cross-section of the U.S. manufacturing sector (see Table A–4). Included are 12 of the largest 20 manufacturing industries in the 1963 Input-Output table based on employment. These figures are even more encouraging when military products (guided missiles, etc.) are excluded from each category. Regional data for these products are not disclosed for national security reasons. There are proportionately more industries omitted among the industries with large employment because these tend to be more diverse, including more than one four-digit SIC industry. Selection of industries primarily in any size group seemed unjustified because such selection could give a more biased picture of the manufacturing sector of the economy than a random selection would if the industries in the size class chosen differed significantly in characteristics to be used in the analysis.

Table A–4. List of 199 industries used.

Number	1963 Input-output study industry number and title		Related SIC code (1957 edition)
001	64.11	Signs and advertising displays	3993
002	14.02	Creamery butter	2021
003	14.04	Cheese, natural and processed	2022
004	14.04	Condensed and evaporated milk	2023
005	14.05	Ice cream and frozen desserts	2024
006	14.06	Fluid milk	2026
007	14.07	Canned and cured sea foods	2031
008	14.08	Canned specialties	2032
009	14.10	Dehydrated food products	2034
010	14.11	Pickles, sauces and salad dressings	2035
011	14.12	Fresh or frozen packaged fish	2036
012	14.15	Prepared feeds for animals and fowls	2042
013	14.16	Rice milling	2044
014	14.17	Wet corn milling	2046
015	14.23	Flavoring extracts and syrups, n.e.c.	2087
016	14.24	Cottonseed oil mills	2091
017	14.25	Soybean oil mills	2092
018	14.26	Vegetable oil mills, n.e.c.	2093

Table A–4 continued.

Number	1963 Input-output study industry number and title	Related SIC code (1957 edition)
019	14.27 Animal and marine fats and oils	2094
020	14.28 Roasted coffee	2095
021	14.29 Shortening and cooking oils	2096
022	14.31 Macaroni and spaghetti	2098
023	14.32 Food preparations, n.e.c.	2099
024	15.02 Tobacco stemming and redrying	2141
025	16.02 Narrow fabric mills	2241
026	16.04 Thread mills	2284
027	17.03 Lace goods	2292
028	17.04 Paddings and upholstery fillings	2293
029	17.05 Processed textile waste	2294
030	17.06 Coated fabrics, not rubberized	2295
031	17.07 Tire cord and fabric	2296
032	17.08 Scouring and combing plants	2297
033	17.09 Cordage and twine	2298
034	17.10 Textile goods, n.e.c.	2299
035	19.01 Curtains and draperies	2391
036	19.02 Housefurnishings, n.e.c.	2392
037	20.01 Logging camps and logging contractors	2411
038	20.02 Sawmills and planing mills, general	2421
039	20.03 Hardwood dimension and flooring	2426
040	20.04 Special product sawmills, n.e.c.	2429
041	20.05 Millwork	2431
042	20.06 Veneer and plywood	2432
043	20.07 Prefabricated wood structures	2433
044	20.08 Wood preserving	2491
045	20.09 Wood products, n.e.c.	2499
046	22.02 Upholstered household furniture	2512
047	22.03 Metal household furniture	2514
048	22.04 Mattresses and bedsprings	2515
049	23.01 Wood office furniture	2521
050	23.04 Wood partitions and fixtures	2541
051	23.05 Metal partitions and fixtures	2542
052	23.06 Venetian blinds and shades	2591
053	23.07 Furniture and fixtures, n.e.c.	2599
054	24.01 Pulp mills	2611
055	24.02 Paper mills, except building paper	2621
056	24.03 Paperboard mills	2631
057	24.04 Envelopes	2642
058	24.05 Sanitary paper products	2647
059	26.02 Periodicals	2721
060	26.04 Miscellaneous publishing	2741
061	28.01 Plastics materials and resins	2821
062	28.03 Cellulosic man-made fibers	2823
063	28.04 Organic fibers, noncellulosic	2824
064	29.03 Toilet preparations	2844
065	30.00 Paints and allied products	2851
066	27.03 Agricultural chemicals, n.e.c.	2879
067	31.02 Paving mixtures and blocks	2591
068	32.01 Tires and inner tubes	3011
069	32.02 Rubber footwear	3021
070	32.04 Miscellaneous plastics products	3079

Table A–4 continued.

Number	1963 Input-output study industry number and title	Related SIC code (1957 edition)
071	34.01 Footwear cut stock	3131
072	35.02 Glass containers	3221
073	36.01 Cement, hydraulic	3241
074	36.02 Brick and structural clay tile	3251
075	36.03 Ceramic wall and floor tile	3253
076	36.04 Clay refractories	3255
077	36.05 Structural clay products, n.e.c.	3259
078	36.08 Porcelain electrical supplies	3264
079	36.09 Pottery products, n.e.c.	3269
080	36.10 Concrete block and brick	3271
081	36.11 Concrete products, n.e.c.	3272
082	36.13 Lime	3274
083	36.15 Cut stone and stone products	3281
084	36.16 Abrasive products	3291
085	36.18 Gaskets and insulations	3293
086	36.19 Minerals, ground or treated	3295
087	36.20 Mineral wool	3296
088	36.21 Nonclay refractories	3297
089	36.22 Nonmetallic mineral products, n.e.c.	3299
090	38.01 Primary copper	3331
091	38.02 Primary lead	3332
092	38.03 Primary zinc	3333
093	38.05 Primary nonferrous metals, n.e.c.	3339
094	38.06 Secondary nonferrous metals	3341
095	38.07 Copper rolling and drawing	3351
096	38.09 Nonferrous rolling and drawing, n.e.c.	3356
097	38.10 Nonferrous wire drawing and insulating	3357
098	38.11 Aluminum castings	3361
099	38.12 Brass, bronze and copper castings	3362
100	38.13 Nonferrous castings, n.e.c.	3369
101	37.03 Iron and steel forgings	3391
102	38.14 Nonferrous forgings	3392
103	37.04 Primary metal products, n.e.c.	3399
104	39.01 Metal cans	3411
105	42.01 Cutlery	3421
106	42.03 Hardware, n.e.c.	3429
107	40.02 Plumbing fittings and brass goods	3432
108	40.03 Heating equipment except electric	3433
109	40.04 Fabricated structural steel	3441
110	40.05 Metal doors, sash and trim	3442
111	40.06 Fabricated plate work (boiler shops)	3443
112	40.08 Architectural metal work	3446
113	40.09 Miscellaneous metal work	3449
114	41.02 Metal stampings	3461
115	42.05 Miscellaneous fabricated wire products	3481
116	39.02 Metal barrels, drums and pails	3491
117	42.07 Steel springs	3493
118	42.09 Collapsible tubes	3496
119	42.10 Metal foil and leaf	3497
120	42.11 Fabricated metal products, n.e.c.	3499
121	43.01 Steam engines and turbines	3511
122	43.02 Internal combustion engines, n.e.c.	3519

Table A–4 continued.

Number	1963 Input-output study industry number and title	Related SIC code (1957 edition)
123	44.00 Farm machinery	3522
124	45.01 Construction machinery	3531
125	45.02 Mining machinery	3532
126	46.01 Elevators and moving stairways	3534
127	46.04 Industrial trucks and tractors	3537
128	47.01 Machine tools, metal cutting types	3541
129	47.02 Machine tools, metal forming types	3542
130	48.01 Food products machinery	3551
131	48.01 Textile machinery	3552
132	48.03 Woodworking machinery	3553
133	48.04 Paper industries machinery	3554
134	48.05 Printing trades machinery	3555
135	48.06 Special industry machinery, n.e.c.	3559
136	49.02 Ball and roller bearings	3562
137	49.03 Blowers and fans	3564
138	49.05 Power transmission equipment	3566
139	49.06 Industrial furnaces and ovens	3567
140	51.01 Computing and related machines	3571
141	51.02 Typewriters	3572
142	51.03 Scales and balances	3576
143	51.04 Office machines, n.e.c.	3579
144	52.02 Commercial laundry equipment	3582
145	52.03 Refrigeration machinery	3585
146	52.04 Measuring and dispensing pumps	3586
147	52.05 Service industry machines, n.e.c.	3589
148	53.01 Electric measuring instruments	3611
149	53.03 Switchgear and switchboard apparatus	3613
150	53.04 Motors and generators	3621
151	53.05 Industrial controls	3622
152	53.06 Welding apparatus	3623
153	53.07 Carbon and graphite products	3624
154	53.08 Electrical industrial apparatus, n.e.c.	3629
155	54.01 Household cooking equipment	3631
156	54.02 Household refrigerators and freezers	3632
157	54.03 Household laundry equipment	3633
158	54.04 Electric housewares and fans	3634
159	54.05 Household vacuum cleaners	3635
160	54.06 Sewing machines	3636
161	54.07 Household appliances, n.e.c.	3639
162	55.01 Electric lamps	3641
163	55.02 Lighting fixtures	3642
164	56.01 Radio and TV receiving sets	3651
165	56.02 Phonograph records	3652
166	56.03 Telephone and telegraph apparatus	3661
167	56.04 Radio and TV communication equipment	3662
168	57.02 Semiconductors	3674
169	57.03 Electronic components, n.e.c.	3679
170	58.01 Storage batteries	3691
171	58.02 Primary batteries, wet and dry	3692
172	58.03 X-ray apparatus and tubes	3693
173	58.04 Engine electrical equipment	3694
174	58.05 Electrical equipment, n.e.c.	3699

Table A–4 continued.

Number	1963 Input-output study industry number and title		Related SIC code (1957 edition)
175	59.01	Truck and bus bodies	3713
176	59.02	Truck trailers	3715
177	59.03	Motor vehicles and parts	3717
178	60.01	Aircraft	3721
179	60.02	Aircraft engines and parts	3722
180	60.03	Aircraft propellers and parts	3723
181	60.04	Aircraft equipment, n.e.c.	3729
182	61.01	Shipbuilding and repairing	3731
183	61.03	Locomotives and parts	3741
184	61.04	Railroad and street cars	3742
185	61.06	Trailer coaches	3791
186	61.07	Transportation equipment, n.e.c.	3799
187	62.01	Engineering and scientific instruments	3811
188	62.02	Mechanical measuring devices	3821
189	63.01	Optical instruments and lenses	3831
190	62.04	Surgical and medical instruments	3841
191	62.05	Surgical appliances and supplies	3842
192	62.06	Dental equipment and supplies	3843
193	63.03	Photographic equipment and supplies	3861
194	64.02	Musical instruments and parts	3931
195	64.03	Games, toys, etc.	3941
196	64.04	Sporting and athletic goods, n.e.c.	3949
197	64.06	Artificial flowers	3962
198	64.08	Brooms and brushes	3981
199	64.09	Hard surface floor covering	3982

NOTES

1. Neither the 1963 Input-Output study industry numbers nor the SIC codes were used in the random selection process because each of these numbering systems appears to be biased: SIC codes appear to be biased toward lower final digits and final digits of 9 while the Input-Output industry numbers appear to be biased toward lower final two-digits.

Section A–3

EXTENT AND CONSEQUENCES OF ERRORS REMAINING IN DATA

The original research plan called for aggregating county populations and areas into regional totals in such a way that a check on the set of codes used to aggregate county employment totals into regional employment totals would also be provided. Technical computational problems delayed completion of this check until after the employment data had been aggregated

Table A-5. Errors made in aggregating county data into regions.

Region number	Name	Number of counties	Error 1: counties omitted	Error 2: counties added
146	St. Louis SMSA	7	Jefferson, Missouri	McDonald, Missouri
227	Norfolk, Virginia-N.C.	19	Chowan, North Carolina	
230	Greensboro, Virginia-N.C.	16	Grayson, Virginia	Lee, Virginia
245	Montgomery, Alabama	19	Tallapoosa, Alabama	Wilcox, Alabama
			Geneva, Alabama	
			Henry, Alabama	
			Houston, Alabama	
248	Columbus, Georgia-Ala.	14	Talbot, Georgia	
250	Birmingham, Ala.-Miss.	32	Calhoun, Mississippi	Catahoula, La.
			Clay, Mississippii	Bienville, La.
			Itawamba, Mississippi	LaFouche, Louisiana
			Lee, Mississippi	Red River, La.
			Monroe, Mississippi	St. John the Baptist Louisiana
			Oktibbeha, Miss.	Tangipahoa, La.
			Pototoc, Mississippi	Vernon, Louisiana
			Prentis, Mississippi	Washington, La.
			Chickasaw, Miss.	
			Choctaw, Mississippi	
			Union, Mississippi	
			Webster, Mississippi	
			Lorondes, Mississippi	
			Noxubee, Mississippi	
251	Memphis, Tenn.-Ark.-Miss.	36	Benton, Mississippi	Avoyelles, La.
			Coahoma, Mississippi	Clairborne, La.
			Marshall, Mississippi	St. James, La.
			Panola, Mississippi	Tensas, Louisiana
			Quitman, Mississippi	Webster, Louisiana
			DeSota, Mississippi	
			Lafayette, Miss.	
			Tate, Mississippi	
			Tippah, Mississippi	
			Tunica, Mississippi	
252	Huntsville, Ala.-Miss.-Tennessee	13	Alcorn, Mississippi	Allen, Louisiana
			Tishomingo, Miss.	
254	Nashville, Tenn.-Ky.	48	Jackson, Tennessee	
256	Bristol, Va.-Tenn.-W.Va.	22	Lee, Virginia	
262	Springfield, Illinois	11	Menard, Illinois	
264	Lafayette, Indiana	8	Caroll, Indiana	Bartholomew, Ill.
265	Indianapolis, Indiana	15	Bartholomew, Indiana	
266	Muncie, Indiana	7	Randolph, Indiana	
277	Saginaw, Michigan	22	Presque Isle, Michigan	Baraga, Michigan
284	Davenport, Rock Island-Moline, Iowa-Illinois	8	Mercer, Illinois	
290	Green Bay, Wisconsin	22	Baraga, Michigan	
			Outagamie, Wisconsin	

Table A–5 continued.

Region number	Name	Number of counties	Error 1: counties omitted	Error 2: counties added
294	LaCrosse, Wisconsin	9	Monroe, Wisconsin	
			Trempealeau, Wisconsin	
297	Grand Forks, N.D.-Minn.	15	Walsh, North Dakota	Ward, North Dakota
298	Minot, N.D.-Montana	16	Ward, North Dakota	
302	Fargo-Moorehead, N.D.-			
	Minnesota	19	Griggs, North Dakota	
308	Sioux City, Iowa-Neb.-			
	South Dakota	29	Pierre, Nebraska	Osborne, Kansas
314	Salina, Kansas	38	Osborne, Kansas	
319	St. Louis, Missouri-	42	St. Genevieve, Mo.	
	Illinois		Monroe, Illinois	
321	Springfield, Mo.-Ka.-	40	Cedar, Missouri	
	Oklahoma-Arkansas		McDonald, Missouri	
330	Abilene, Texas	15	Knox, Texas	Milam, Texas
334	Austin, Texas	15	Milam, Texas	
337	Shreveport, Louisiana	7	Clairborne, Louisiana	
			Bienville, Louisiana	
			Webster, Louisiana	
			Red River, Louisiana	
338	Monroe, Louisiana	17	Tensas, Louisiana	
			Avoyelles, Louisiana	
			Catahoula, Louisiana	
339	Greenville, Miss.-Ark.	23	Tallahatchie, Miss.	
342	Mobile, Ala.-Miss.	10	Wilcox, Alabama	
343	New Orleans, La.-Miss.	31	St. James, Louisiana	
			St. John the Baptist, La.	
			La Fouche, Louisiana	
			Tangipahoa, Louisiana	
			Washington, Louisiana	
344	Lake Charles, La.	12	Allen, Louisiana	
			Vernon, Louisiana	
350	El Paso, Texas-N.M.	16	Dona Ana, New Mexico	
353	Denver, Colo.-Neb.	21	Chase, Nebraska	
			Dundy, Nebraska	
			Perkins, Nebraska	
354	Grand Junction, Colorado-	19	San Juan, New Mexico	
	Utah-New Mexico		San Juan, Utah	
			Grand, Utah	
357	Idaho Falls, Idaho-Wyo.	22	Teton, Wyoming	
366	Las Vegas, Nevada-Utah	8	Beaver, Utah	
			Garfield, Utah	
			Iron, Utah	
			Kane, Utah	
			Washington, Utah	
367	Phoenix, Arizona	8	Gila, Arizona	Greenlee, Arizona
368	Tucson, Arizona	4	Greenlee, Arizona	
376	San Francisco-Oakland,			
	California	6	Santa Cruz, California	

and correlation coefficients produced and tested. When the check was made, a total of 113 aggregation errors were found in 42 regions. (See Table A–5 for a summary of these errors.) The number of errors would be cause for more concern if it were not for the facts that 1. only one SMSA is affected and 2. an examination of the affected regions indicates that most are not greatly affected. Two basic types of errors were found. The first and least consequential occurred when a county was omitted from a region either through oversight or through being assigned an incorrect code that corresponded to no country. Twenty-four of the errors of this type were found; most of these omitted counties have very few employees in the manufacturing industries included in this study so that their omission was judged to have a negligible impact on the results.

The second type of error occurred when a county was assigned an incorrect code which represented another county, causing omission of the county with no further consequences when the region with the incorrect code had a higher number than the region in which that code was supposed to appear. (The aggregation algorithm placed county observations in only the lowest numbered region in which it encountered the county code.) This occurred in 17 cases. When the region with the incorrectly coded county had a lower number than the region in which the county with that code belonged, the result was the inclusion of the data for an incorrect county in the first region, and omission of data for correct counties from both the first and second counties.

Consideration of each individual error permitted the conclusion to be drawn that overall results for the study were not significantly affected by the coding errors and that recomputation with the corrected codes was not justified.

Table A–6. Estimated and reported employment totals for selected Sic's and SMSA's.

Industry		S.M.S.A.		Employment	
Sic	Number	Name	Region Number	Recorded	Estimated
2087	15	Chicago	34	1634	1550
		Los Angeles	99	340	319
		New York	117	1294	1561
		Philadelphia	129	452	462
		St. Louis	146	469	531
		San Francisco	152	184	252
2293	28	New York	117	287	258
		Philadelphia	129	1754	342
2297	32	Philadelphia	129	3249	595
2541	50	Cleveland	36	199	219
		Detroit	48	327	355
		Los Angeles	99	2400	2438
		New York	117	3240	3248
		Philadelphia	129	867	880
		St. Louis	146	803	828
		San Francisco	152	826	830
2542	51	Cleveland	36	1417	1370
		Detroit	48	374	376
		Los Angeles	99	851	981
		New York	117	2158	2154
		Philadelphia	129	1055	1124
		St. Louis	146	200	199
		San Francisco	152	340	359
2591	52	Los Angeles	99	409	522
		New York	117	1221	1439
		San Francisco	152	121	133
2851	65	Baltimore	17	1146	2737
		Cleveland	36	3436	3224
		Detroit	48	2784	2959
		Los Angeles	99	3826	3959
		Milwaukee	108	846	704
		New York	117	2834	2633
		Newark	118	3303	3146
		Philadelphia	129	3123	4508
		Pittsburg	131	1246	1347
		St. Louis	146	1333	1492
		San Francisco	152	2126	1999
2951	67	Philadelphia	129	235	233
3079	70	Baltimore	17	2219	3651
		Cleveland	36	2149	2225
		Detroit	48	3575	3676
		Los Angeles	99	10342	10477
		New York	117	12767	12610
		Newark	118	5534	5416
		Philadelphia	129	4317	4173
		St. Louis	146	1769	1523
		San Francisco	152	1121	1173

Source: Estimated industry employment based on *Location of Manufacturing Plants by County, Industry and Employment Size* [51]; reported industry employment from *Industry Profiles* [54].

Appendix B

Section B–1

This appendix demonstrates that standard computational procedures used
for calculating coefficients of correlation will produce biased results unless
observations containing zero values for all variables are omitted. Furthermore it is shown that such observations are likely to be present when data
such as those in the present study are used in a disaggregated form.

In the following paragraphs the theoretical effects of zero observations
on coefficients of correlations are stated and illustrative examples using
data from the Census of Manufactures are presented.

The sample correlation coefficient, r, is often calculated as

$$\frac{n\Sigma xy - \Sigma x \Sigma y}{\{[n\Sigma x^2 - (\Sigma x)^2][n\Sigma y^2 - (\Sigma y)^2]\}^{\frac{1}{2}}}$$

where the summations are over all values of the two variables, x and y, and
n is the sample size. It is clear that the value of r varies with n provided all
other magnitudes remain unchanged. As n increases without bound the
value of r^2 approaches a limit of $\frac{(\Sigma xy)^2}{\Sigma x^2 \Sigma y^2}$, and thus the value of r will
approach the (positive) square root of this limit from below.[1]

In addition to increasing the value of r, larger values of n will directly
influence hypothesis tests regarding r. Provided the joint distribution of x
and y is bivariate normal, the hypothesis that the population correlation
coefficient ρ is equal to zero may be tested by constructing a t statistic as

$\frac{r\sqrt{n-2}}{\sqrt{1-r^2}}$ and comparing with tabulated values of t with $n-2$ degrees of
freedom for any desired level of significance. This value is seen to vary
directly with n as does r. Tests of the hypothesis that ρ equals some value

other than zero are usually performed using Fisher's z-transformation and constructing the standard normal deviate, $Z = \dfrac{z - \zeta H}{\sigma z}$, which is compared with tabulated values for any desired level of significance. Because $z = 1/2 \ln \dfrac{1 + r}{1 - r}$, $\zeta H = 1/2 \ln \dfrac{1 + \rho_H}{1 - \rho_H}$ where ρ_H is the hypothesized value of ρ, and $\sigma_z = \dfrac{1}{\sqrt{n - 3}}$, Z also will vary directly with n. Thus variations in the magnitude of r with variations in n are not only *not* offset by inverse variations in the likelihood of rejecting all hypotheses about ρ, but such variations are magnified.

A correlation coefficient is used in this study as a measure of the strength of the geographic association between two industries where the magnitudes correlated are measures of employment for each industry in a number of geographic regions as has been done by Florence [13], McCarty *et al.* [34], Richter [42] and Streit [47].

In the following example a set of regions is initially defined as 20 of the Office of Business Economics' 173 economic regions of the United States.

Table B–1. Estimated number of employees in four SIC industries in 20 OBE regions.

Region		(1)	(2)	(3)	(4)
OBE number	Name	SIC 357	SIC 371	SIC 3571	SIC 3715
009	Buffalo, N.Y.	383	16723	346	0
012	Binghamton, N.Y.	5689	3906	3138	0
017	Baltimore, Md.	174	8167	131	12
026	Charlotte, N.C.	415	826	69	0
029	Columbia, S.C.	408	37	377	31
032	*Augusta, Ga.	6	37	0	0
043	*Columbus, Ga.	6	37	0	0
044	*Atlanta, Ga.	100	11816	0	0
048	*Chattanooga, Tenn.	0	24	0	0
058	Champaign, Ill.	6	383	6	0
064	Columbus, Ohio	236	2171	0	31
079	Davenport, Ia.	155	342	0	69
080	Cedar Rapids, Ia.	0	100	69	0
106	*Des Moines, Ia.	6	380	0	0
122	*Amarillo, Tex.	6	93	0	0
129	*Austin, Tex.	0	167	0	0
140	*Beaumont, Tex.	0	12	0	0
146	Albuquerque, N.M.	31	118	31	100
148	Denver, Colo.	67	1088	55	377
159	Boise City, Id.	0	61	0	6

*Indicates a region in which neither SIC 3571 nor SIC 3715 is located.
Source: estimates are based on data contained in the *Census of manufactures, location of manufacturing plants by county, industry and employment size* (1963) [51].

The industries used here are Office, Computing and Accounting Machines (1957 SIC code 357) and Motor Vehicles and Parts (1957 SIC code 371). The employment estimates for each of these industries in the 20 regions are shown in columns (1) and (2) of Table B–1. The coefficient of correlation for the two distributions is .1330 and the value of t is .5692.

The data were then disaggregated spatially by dividing each of the OBE regions into a segment consisting of a Standard Metropolitan Statistical Area within the OBE region and a second segment consisting of the area within the OBE region but outside of the SMSA. The employment estimates for the two industries in the 40 new regions are shown in columns (1) and (2) of Table B–2. Using the same calculating procedure as above, the correlation coefficient between the distributions of employment estimates in the two industries using the spatially disaggregated data is .0817 and the value of t is .5054. Note, however, that the disaggregation resulted in five observations for which the estimated employment in both industries is zero. Further disaggregation down to the county level and below would produce still more such paired-zero observations. The effect of paired-zero observations in this case is to increase the value of r and t in a spurious fashion. The fact that neither industry has located in some geographic areas should not lead one to conclude that the two industries tend to associate themselves with each other spatially. Such a conclusion would permit the inflation of the coefficient of correlation to the limit described above simply by finer geographic subdivisions contributing pairs of zero observations which increase n but do not affect any other magnitudes. Omitting the five paired zero observations yields a value of r of .0661 which is 19% lower than the value with the paired zeroes included and reduces the value of t to .3804.

The original data were next disaggregated from three-digit SIC code industries to four-digit SIC code industries. Columns (2) and (3) of Table B–1 show the employment estimates for Computing and Related Machines (SIC code 3571) and Truck Trailers (SIC code 3715). The correlation coefficient and value of t for these two distributions are, respectively, $-.0942$ and $-.4016$ with the eight paired zero observations included and $-.1963$ and $-.6330$ without them (a reduction in the value of r of 108%).

Thus, the theoretical effect on r and t of increasing n without changing any other magnitudes has been found to occur when Census of Manufactures data are disaggregated in either their spatial or industrial dimensions. In some situations paired zeroes might be quite meaningful and, if so, then increases in r because of such observation would not be at all spurious. For example, correlations between measures of incomes and education levels should be influenced by pairs of zero observations. In the example above and in this study, however, the increase in the value of r can be considered spurious and paired zeroes must be omitted from the calculations in the correlation coefficients in such cases.[2]

Table B–2. Estimated number of employees in four SIC industries in 20 SMSA's and surrounding areas.

Region	SIC 357 (1)	SIC 371 (2)	SIC 3571 (3)	SIC 3715 (4)
Buffalo, N.Y. SMSA	37	15717	0	0
Surrounding Area	346	519	346	0
Binghamton, N.Y. SMSA	2792	6	2786	0
Surrounding Area	2897	3900	352	0
Baltimore, Md. SMSA	168	5523	131	6
Surrounding Area	6	2644	0	6
Charlotte, N.C. SMSA	0	93	0	0
Surrounding Area	415	733	69	0
Columbia, S.C. SMSA	31	6	0	0
Surrounding Area	377	31	377	31
Augusta, Ga. SMSA	31	0	0	0
*Surrounding Area	0	0	0	0
Columbus, Ga. SMSA	6	37	0	0
*Surrounding Area	0	0	0	0
Atlanta, Ga. SMSA	100	10928	0	0
Surrounding Area	0	888	0	0
Chattanooga, Tenn. SMSA	0	12	0	0
Surrounding Area	0	12	0	0
Champaign, Ill. SMSA	6	37	6	0
Surrounding Area	0	346	0	0
Columbus, Ohio SMSA	236	2065	0	0
Surrounding Area	0	106	0	31
Davenport, Ia. SMSA	155	273	0	69
Surrounding Area	0	69	0	0
Cedar Rapids, Ia. SMSA	0	100	0	69
*Surrounding Area	0	0	0	0
Des Moines, Ia. SMSA	6	143	0	0
Surrounding Area	0	237	0	0
Amarillo, Tex. SMSA	6	87	0	0
Surrounding Area	0	6	0	0
Austin, Tex. SMSA	0	167	0	0
*Surrounding Area	0	0	0	0
Beaumont, Tex. SMSA	0	12	0	0
*Surrounding Area	0	0	0	0
Albuquerque, N.M. SMSA	31	112	31	100
Surrounding Area	0	6	0	0
Denver, Colo. SMSA	67	1051	55	377
Surrounding Area	0	37	0	0
Boise City, Id. SMSA	0	55	0	0
Surrounding Area	0	6	0	0

*Indicates a region in which neither SIC 357 nor SIC 371 is located.
Indicates a region in which neither SIC 3571 nor 3715 is located.
Source: estimates are based on data contained in the Census of manufactures, location of manufacturing plants by county, industry and employment size (1963) [51].

The following are two examples of studies in which bias of the type identified above may have influenced the results. Others could have been cited but these serve as indicators of one class of study likely to be subject to this bias.

1. Richter [41] used the 1958 Census of Manufactures to construct a matrix of employment estimates for two- and three-digit SIC industries in a group of large SMSA's. Because this matrix contained a significant number of zero observations, measures of geographic association for some pairs of industries, calculated using this data, may have been biased. Utilization of more disaggregated data would certainly increase the potential for bias.

2. Czamanski [9] computed four correlation coefficients for every pair of industries in an expanded form of the 1958 Input-Output Study using the inter-industry transactions as his data. Even at his level of aggregation (89 industries) many paired zero observations were included in his calculations, possibly biasing his final results. Any attempt to apply his methods to a more disaggregated set of data would certainly encounter significant bias unless paired zeroes were discarded.

The preceding paragraphs have shown how straight-forward application of computational formulas for the coefficient of correlation to data containing pairs of zero observations can lead to biased estimates of these measures. The occurrence of pairs of zero observations was shown to be likely when spatial industrial data such as that used in the present study are disaggregated spatially or industrially. The computational algorithm used in this study provides for the elimination of paired zero observations when such observations are not meaningful.

NOTES

1. $\displaystyle \lim_{n \to \infty} r^2 = \lim_{n \to \infty} \frac{\left[\Sigma xy - \dfrac{\Sigma x \Sigma y}{n} \right]^2}{\left[\Sigma x^2 - \dfrac{(\Sigma x)^2}{n} \right]\left[\Sigma y^2 - \dfrac{(\Sigma y)^2}{n} \right]} = \frac{(\Sigma xy)^2}{\Sigma x^2 \Sigma y^2}$

   which must be ≥ 0 because all quantities are squared, and must also be ≤ 1 by the Schwarz inequality.

2. In the example used the addition of paired zero observations has obviously caused the joint distributions of the variables to depart from normality and thus invalidates any tests of r. In some applications the number of paired zero observations added may be small enough, however, not to significantly alter the joint distribution, especially if the distributions of nonzero observations have means close to zero.

Section B–2

FACTOR ANALYSIS IDENTIFICATION OF INDUSTRIAL COMPLEXES

Czamanski's method may be described, using the notation of Chapter 2, as follows:

1. Four correlation coefficients for every pair of industries, k and l, are computed as follows:

   a. The correlation between $\dfrac{Y_{i,k}}{\sum\limits_{j} Y_{k,j}}$ and $\dfrac{Y_{i,l}}{\sum\limits_{j} Y_{l,j}}$ for $i = 1, \ldots, 199$, gives a measure of the similarity of the two industries' input structures. To correct the deficiency noted in Chapter 3, this should be changed to the correlation between $\dfrac{Y_{i,k}}{I_k}$ and $\dfrac{Y_{i,l}}{I_l}$. Use of the first measures gives significance to similarity of industries k and l as viewed by all of their suppliers as a group while the second emphasizes similarity of the two industries in terms of similar proportionate reliance on the group of suppliers.

   b. The correlation between $\dfrac{Y_{k,j}}{\sum\limits_{j} Y_{k,j}}$ and $\dfrac{Y_{l,j}}{\sum\limits_{j} Y_{l,j}}$ for $j = 1, \ldots, 199$ gives a measure of the similarity of the output structures of the two industries. High values would indicate that the relative importance of different demanders to each of the two industries is similar.

   c. The correlation between $\dfrac{Y_{i,k}}{\sum\limits_{j} Y_{k,j}}$ and $\dfrac{Y_{l,i}}{\sum\limits_{j} Y_{l,j}}$ for $i = 1, \ldots, n$ gives a measure of the degree to which the proportionate distribution of industry k's inputs resembles the proportionate distribution for industry l's output.

   d. The correlation between $\dfrac{Y_{k,j}}{\sum\limits_{j} Y_{k,j}}$ and $\dfrac{Y_{i,l}}{\sum\limits_{j} Y_{l,j}}$ for $i,j = 1, \ldots, 199$ gives a measure of the degree to which the proportionate distribution of industry l's inputs resembles the proportionate distribution for industry k's output.

In all of these measures one might be more satisfied if the correlations were computed over all values of i or $j = 1, \ldots, 199$ *except* for i or $j = k$ or l. The justification for omitting own proportions can be illustrated by noting that the second correlation coefficient, the one measuring similarity of output structures, would be higher, other flows being equal, for two industries that do not trade with each other at all than for two which have large flows to each other but consume little of their own products. If one wanted to interpret the second case as exhibiting more, rather than less, similarity of output structure than the first, the correlation might be over the pairs

$$\frac{Y_{k,j}}{\sum\limits_{j} Y_{k,j}}, \frac{Y_{l,j}}{\sum\limits_{j} Y_{l,j}} \quad \text{for } j = 1, \ldots, n \text{ and } j \neq k \text{ or } l; \quad \frac{Y_{k,l}}{\sum\limits_{j} Y_{k,j}}, \frac{Y_{l,k}}{\sum\limits_{j} Y_{l,j}}; \text{ and}$$

$$\frac{Y_{l,l}}{\sum\limits_{j} Y_{l,j}}, \frac{Y_{k,k}}{\sum\limits_{j} Y_{k,j}}.$$

2. A square matrix, R, is formed with its elements being the largest of the four correlation coefficients described above for each pair of industries, except where none are significantly different from zero or a diagonal element is considered and a zero is entered. It is unfortunate that this procedure automatically eliminates at this step three-fourths of the information already obtained, especially if some of the discarded correlation coefficients are large. Some sort of aggregation of the four coefficients might be more desirable.

3. All null vectors are removed from the matrix, removing from consideration as part of a complex those industries not linked with any others.

4. The ratios of the characteristic roots to the trace of the R matrix are then called Indexes of Association. A large value indicates an industrial complex. The characteristic roots are also interpretable as variances (in orthogonal regression), determining the degree of affinity of industries forming a complex. (The characteristic vectors associated with the characteristic roots identify the industries belonging to a complex.)

Table B–3. *Number of separate regions in which each industry appears.*

Industry Number	Number of Regions	Industry number	Number of regions	Industry number	Number of regions	Industry number	Number of regions
1	341	51	123	101	94	151	108
2	147	52	202	102	23	152	58
3	142	53	116	103	142	153	29
4	120	54	30	104	112	154	72
5	280	55	98	105	64	155	39
6	368**	56	126	106	186	156	26
7	68	57	68	107	84	157	27
8	93	58	48	108	173	158	116
9	43	59	283	109	293	159	21
10	180	60	215	110	270	160	26
11	85	61	135	111	277	161	52
12	343	62	17	112	260	162	41
13	17	63	19	113	187	163	139
14	34	64	120	114	220	164	85
15	133	65	229	115	213	165	42
16	78	66	153	116	69	166	41
17	70	67	236	117	45	167	181
18	30	68	87	118	22	168	40
19	246	69	31	119	28	169	210
20	104	70	288	120	224	170	111
21	55	71	56	121	16	171	35
22	65	72	62	122	75	172	24
23	322	73	116	123	273	173	86
24	34	74	202	124	195	174	111
25	76	75	57	125	93	175	190
26	26	76	54	126	63	176	108
27	22	77	82	127	122	177	266
28	77	78	44	128	131	178	56
29	55	79	134	129	103	179	83
30	56	80	348	130	171	180	12
31	15	81	358	131	97	181	136
32	31	82	69	132	102	182	92
33	76	83	211	133	71	183	16
34	60	84	95	134	97	184	44
35	161	85	85	135	213	185	143
36	166	86	167	136	61	186	195
37	282	87	67	137	91	187	127
38	334	88	54	138	126	188	150
39	166	89	118	139	71	189	75
40	134	90	17	140	69	190	93
41	344	91	8*	141	15	191	182
42	145	92	16	142	47	192	90
43	212	93	28	143	62	193	91
44	157	94	111	144	60	194	105
45	308	95	46	145	174	195	162
46	233	96	60	146	33	196	271
47	116	97	85	147	141	197	108
48	260	98	185	148	120	179	198
49	51	99	144	149	110	199	15
50	239	100	100	150	121		

*Indicates the minimum number.
**Indicates the maximum number.

Appendix C

Section C–1

SUMMARY OF BILATERAL LINKAGES AND ASSOCIATIONS BY INDUSTRY

This section and Table C–1 together explain the entries in Table C–2 which summarize the bilateral linkage and association relationships for each industry. (This information for all 199 industries is aggregated in Table 5–2.) The linkage and association relationships between any pair of industries can be described by a number from 0 to 31. These numbers appear in the left-hand column of Table C–1. Each number is the sum of the values assigned for each kind of linkage and geographic association for the industry. A zero indicates that the industry pair has no significant relationships. A value of 1 is for a demand link, 2 is for a supply link, 4 is for a strong demand link, 8 is for a strong supply link, and 16 is for a geographic association. Thus, a value of 11, for example, means that one industry is linked to another industry in demand and supply and strongly in supply and they are not geographically associated with each other.

The numbers at the tops of the columns of Table C–2 are those numbers which represent sets of relationships between industry pairs actually found in the study. Note that no sets of relationships that would be described by the numbers 4, 8, 9, 12, 13, 14, 20, 21, 24, 25, 26, 28, or 30 were found to exist between any of the industry pairs. The entries in Table C–2 show the number of second industries with which the industry in the left-hand column has sets of relationships described by the numbers at the top of each column. Thus, for example, industry 10 has a set of relationships that could be described by the number 3 (demand and supply links only, as indicated in Table C–1) with two other industries. In addition industry 10 is geographically associated only (number 16) with three other industries.

The column in Table C–2 headed T_1 gives the total number of other industries with which the left-hand column industry is linked but not associated. The T_2 column shows the number of industries with which the left-hand column industry is both linked and associated.

Table C–1. Coding of linkage and association data.

Value assigned to industry pair	Demand link	Supply link	Strong demand	Strong supply	Geographic association
0	0	0	0	0	0
1	1	0	0	0	0
2	0	2	0	0	0
3	1	2	0	0	0
4	0	0	4	0	0
5	1	0	4	0	0
6	0	2	4	0	0
7	1	2	4	0	0
8	0	0	0	8	0
9	1	0	0	8	0
10	0	2	0	8	0
11	1	2	0	8	0
12	0	0	4	8	0
13	1	0	4	8	0
14	0	2	4	8	0
15	1	2	4	8	0
16	0	0	0	0	16
17	1	0	0	0	16
18	0	2	0	0	16
19	1	2	0	0	16
20	0	0	4	0	16
21	1	0	4	0	16
22	0	2	4	0	16
23	1	2	4	0	16
24	0	0	0	8	16
25	1	0	0	8	16
26	0	2	0	8	16
27	1	2	0	8	16
28	0	0	4	8	16
29	1	0	4	8	16
30	0	2	4	8	16
31	1	2	4	8	16

Table C-2. Summary of bilateral linkages and associations by industry[a].

Industry	1	2	3	5	6	7	10	11	15	T₁	16	17	18	19	22	23	27	30	31	T₂
1		1				1			1	3	54					1				1
2			1			1			1	3	0									0
3									1	1	0									0
4			1			2			1	4	0									0
5		1								1	50									0
6									4	4	51								1	1
7		1	1			3			1	3	3									1
8		1	1			1			1	6	0									0
9		1	2						1	3	0									0
10		2				2				4	3					1				1
11								1	1	2	0									0
12										1	0									0
13										0	0									0
14	1	4	3			2		1		11	0	1				1				2
15		1								1	40									0
16		3	1			1			3	6	0									0
17		1	3			1			2	5	0									0
18		1								4	1									0
19	1	1							1	2	44			1						1
20	1	2	3	1		2				3	3								1	1
21		2	1						1	9	1	1				1				1
22		1								2	35									0
23		1				2				1	48	1		1		1				3
24		2	1			1			1	6	0									0
25	2								1	3	0							1		1
26	2								1	1	1									0
27		1								6	0									0
28	2	1				2			1	1	0									0
29									1	11	0									0
30	1	1	3			5			1	1	0									0
31									1	2	0									0
32		2									1									0

33	34	35	36	37	38	39	40	41	42	43	44	45	46	47	48	49	50	51	52	53	54	55	56	57	58	59	60	61	62	63	64	65	66	67	68
0	1	1	3	2	0	0	1	1	0	0	5	0	3	1	0	2	4	0	1	0	0	0	0	0	1	1	0	0	0	0	8	18	0	0	0
		3																			1														
	1					1		1			1	1																							
								1																											
1			2			1		2								1	1											10							
				1			2	1		1	2																	6							
1						1									1													2							
0	5	24	30	0	0	0	1	14	1	0	0	20	0	40	17	0	41	26	0	42	0	0	0	41	0	20	39	0	0	0	31	39	0	20	0
6	4	1	2	7	21	8	4	3	16	1	1	14	4	3	7	2	3	2	4	1	4	13	8	0	0	0	1	29	6	7	1	27	0	1	10
			1	4	8		5			2	3					1		2	5							7	2	2							
	1		2			1	1											1	1							1	1	1							
																											1								
1	1		1	7	3		1	3		2	1	1	2	1	2	1	1	1			1					2		4				4			
1			1																																
										1	1																								
1	2		1	1	2	3	3	1	2		5		1	2		1	1				1	4	2			11	2	2	1	10		6			
2	2		3	1	1	1	3	1		3			1	1		2		1	3						1	8	1	1		9		1			
2			1			2		2			1						2	2								4									

Table C–2. (cont.)

Industry	1	2	3	5	6	7	10	11	15	T1	16	17	18	19	22	23	27	30	31	T2
69		1								1	1									0
70	5	7	10			8		3	5	38	35	2	3	11		8			5	29
71										0	0									0
72	1	2	1			3			1	8	0									0
73								1	1	2	0									0
74		1								1	0									0
75										0	0									0
76		3	1							4	0									0
77		1								1	0									0
78							1			1	0									0
79										0	3									0
80										0	31		1							1
81		1								1	28		1							1
82		1	1							2	0									0
83			1							1	1									0
84	3	7	2			2			1	15	0									0
85	2	3	1							6	22	1	1	1						3
86		5	1						1	7	3									0
87	1	3	4			1				9	0									0
88			1					2		3	0									0
89	1	2							1	4	6			1						1
90	1	3	2					1	5	12	0									0
91	1	2	4					4		11	0									0
92		1	5					1	1	8	0									0
93		4	5						2	11	0									0
94		1		1					4	6	52									0
95	2	11	17			1		1	3	35	0									0
96	1	6	17	1				1	2	27	0									0
97	2	9	10			2			3	28	3		2							2
98	3	7	11			1			2	24	1									0
99	3	4	7							14	12									0

	100	101	102	103	104	105	106	107	108	109	110	111	112	113	114	115	116	117	118	119	120	121	122	123	124	125	126	127	128	129	130	131	132	133	134
	2	0	0	0	4	0	0	0	0	3	2	1	0	2	14	11	1	1	0	0	4	0	1	0	2	1	0	0	0	0	1	0	0	0	1
											1						1																		
														1		1																			
			1											2				2	1																
	1		3							1	1		9	6	1			1			1														
	1								1		1	1	3						1	1			1												1
									1			1	1		1			1																	
	36	4	0	23	29	2	0	0	1	14	36	5	43	26	28	43	12	2	0	0	56	0	3	0	14	2	3	1	0	24	8	0	4	0	45
	14	21	6	8	8	2	22	4	10	7	2	18	0	2	43	22	3	4	1	3	15	6	9	15	17	9	2	3	8	4	4	5	3	2	1
		3		3				1		1			2			1	3	1			1	1			1	1		1	1						
	1			2	1					2		1			1						1														
																		1																	
	2	1		2	1	2	1	2	1	2					10	2		2	1		3	1	2	4	3			2		1					
				1						1						1																			
														1																					
	7	11	2	4	2	1	12	2	7	2	10		21	9	2		6	1	4	5	6	3		2	4	4	2	3	2	1					
	2	5	4	2	1		3		1	2	1	4	2	9	4	3		1	6	3		3	6	4		1			1	1					
	2	1	2			1				1			3	2			1			2	1	1	1		1										

Table C–2. (cont.)

Industry	1	2	3	5	6	7	10	11	15	T1	16	17	18	19	22	23	27	30	31	T2
135	2	2	5			2			1	12	9									0
136	3	4	16			3			1	27	0									0
137		1	4							5	0									0
138		4	13			9			2	28	0									1
139	1					1				1	21			1						1
140		1	3						2	7	4									0
141		2							1	3	0									0
142			1							1	9									0
143			1							1	9									0
144										0	0									0
145		4	5						4	14	0									0
146		2	1							3	0									0
147			2							2	36									2
148	2	1	4			1			2	6	7		1	1						2
149	2	3	5			5			2	12	12		1	1						2
150	4	9	21			2			6	45	0									0
151	2	2	10			1			3	19	2									1
152		1	2						1	5	2									0
153		4	3							7	0									0
154	2	4	2	1						8	0		1							1
155			1			1				3	0									0
156			1			1			4	6	0									0
157		1	3						1	5	0									0
158	1	1	1			2			1	6	7									0
159										0	1									0
160									1	1	1									0
161	2	2	2			2				8	14			1						1
162	1		4							5	0									0
163	1	1	1							2	51									0
164	1	1	2						1	5	27			1						1
165						1				2	0									0

Industry																				Total
166	2	4	3			2			10	15		2	2					2		0
167	1	2	6			1			13	32		1	3							7
168	3	3	6						11	0		1	1					4		1
169	2	3	8						16	44		1								7
170		1	2						5	0										0
171			1			1			2	0										0
172			4					1	1	2										1
173		1	2						7	0										0
174		1	1			4			3	0										0
175		2	2			1			3	0										0
176		3	16						3	0								1		0
177	2	1	1						29	1								1		1
178			3						3	0										0
179		4	3						10	9										0
180		1	8						4	0										0
181		2	3						13	0			1							2
182		3	2	1					5	0										0
183	1		3						3	0										0
184		2	3						6	0			1							0
185						1			1	0										1
186			3			3			4	2		1								0
187		7	3						16	9		1	1							2
188			1						3	12										0
189			3						4	0										1
190	1	1	2			1			5	5		1	1							2
191		1	1						1	14										1
192	2		2			3			5	26										0
193						1			1	4										1
194	2	1							3	26										0
195	2								3	25										1
196	2								0	5										1
197			1						4	16										0
198	2	1		1					1	13										0
199										0										0
Totals	111	318	524	9	5	180	2	34	182	1900	15	42	69	1	28	2	1	22		0

Section C–2

This section explains Table C–3 on the following pages which presents the results of the examination of the effect of cluster size on geographic associations described in Chapter 4. The correlation coefficients, with their sample sizes (after omitting paired zero observations) in parentheses, are arranged by original industry pairs. The nine coefficients for each original industry pair are arranged with the coefficients between the two new large industries at the lower right and the coefficients between the two new small industries at the upper left. The subdivisions of the industry whose number is listed first above each group are in the rows and the subdivisions of the industry whose number is listed second are in the columns. The number in parentheses following the listing of the two industries is the correlation between these two original industries. For example, the correlation between industries 47 and 67 is .587. The correlation between industry 47's small subdivision and industry 67's medium subdivision is − .283 and the sample size for this calculation was 136.

Table C-3. Correlations between employment estimates for three subdivisions of ten industries.

Band 1

	47,67 (r = .587)			47,70 (r = .825)			47,114 (r = .698)			47,126 (r = .268)		
	-.267 (176)	-0.283 (136)	.383 (153)	.115 (264)	-.068 (252)	-.084 (259)	.058 (215)	-.131 (203)	-.137 (196)	-.258 (113)	-.344 (062)	.132 (071)
	-.399 (115)	-.796 (059)	-.554 (079)	-.243 (091)	-.652 (028)	-.516 (049)	-.298 (084)	-.398 (038)	-.581 (017)	-.247 (084)	-.581 (013)	.090 (034)
	-.253 (114)	-.108 (059)	.443 (071)	-.247 (092)	-.361 (026)	.739 (040)	-.155 (092)	.570 (041)	-.571 (026)	-.142 (079)	-.355 (011)	.031 (032)

Band 2

	47,134 (r = .749)			47,144 (r = .253)			47,157 (r = .026)			47,169 (r = .777)		
	-.162 (122)	-.045 (085)	-.136 (097)	-.214 (100)	-.515 (043)	-.131 (061)	-.206 (090)	-.466 (023)	-.227 (040)	-.127 (205)	.014 (173)	-.119 (185)
	-.248 (083)	-.833 (015)	-.342 (035)	-.056 (080)	-.860 (013)	-.305 (034)	-.021 (079)	-.965 (013)	-.285 (033)	-.248 (090)	-.940 (027)	-.432 (045)
	-.191 (085)	-.591 (017)	.721 (032)	-.260 (088)	-.613 (026)	.020 (042)	-.034 (084)	-.751 (018)	-.254 (035)	-.188 (091)	-.379 (029)	.677 (045)

Band 3

	47,170 (r = .418)			67,70 (r = .673)			67,114 (r = .535)			67,126 (r = .221)		
	-.243 (132)	-.052 (080)	-.214 (098)	-.116 (273)	.009 (261)	-.100 (270)	-.096 (239)	-.073 (212)	-.174 (215)	-.328 (166)	-.296 (093)	-.089 (091)
	-.277 (088)	-.876 (025)	-.444 (043)	-.408 (144)	-.603 (067)	-.458 (070)	-.401 (138)	-.637 (060)	-.087 (060)	-.380 (136)	-.808 (059)	-.100 (057)
	-.127 (089)	-.485 (025)	.237 (043)	-.388 (147)	-.646 (072)	.582 (059)	-.383 (146)	-.638 (066)	.329 (063)	-.083 (131)	-.751 (055)	.039 (056)

Table C–3 continued.

67,134 (r = .548)			67,144 (r = .180)			67,157 (r = –.015)			67,169 (r = .619)		
–.313 (183)	–.220 (117)	–.190 (114)	–.163 (146)	–.567 (086)	–.287 (080)	–.307 (140)	–.436 (065)	–.180 (064)	–.138 (232)	–.151 (194)	–.098 (193)
–.221 (133)	–.796 (059)	–.198 (058)	–.300 (133)	–.367 (055)	–.194 (058)	–.131 (131)	–.716 (056)	–.280 (057)	–.283 (140)	–.864 (068)	–.308 (067)
–.311 (138)	–.621 (059)	.492 (057)	–.286 (141)	–.683 (066)	–.130 (065)	–.229 (135)	–.631 (061)	–.319 (060)	–.362 (146)	–.644 (067)	.459 (067)

67,170 (r = .268)			70,114 (r = .767)			70,126 (r = .353)			70,134 (r = .866)		
–.341 (178)	–.324 (113)	–.222 (113)	.106 (284)	.287 (195)	–.160 (205)	–.010 (264)	–.149 (067)	.044 (066)	.086 (267)	–.047 (093)	–.185 (092)
–.283 (141)	–.778 (066)	–.456 (067)	–.086 (253)	–.830 (031)	–.370 (026)	–.130 (252)	–.934 (029)	–.051 (022)	.064 (248)	–.940 (029)	–.445 (025)
.335 (143)	–.666 (067)	.048 (065)	–.021 (257)	–.658 (039)	.575 (038)	–.060 (248)	–.397 (024)	.042 (022)	–.113 (255)	–.636 (029)	.854 (022)

70,144 (r = .351)			70,157 (r = .071)			70,169 (r = .865)			70,170 (r = .348)		
–.076 (261)	–.584 (053)	–.313 (050)	–.040 (252)	–.540 (036)	–.282 (030)	.089 (287)	–.098 (183)	–.120 (182)	–.038 (264)	–.210 (091)	–.235 (090)
.022 (248)	–.923 (027)	–.287 (023)	.040 (247)	–.815 (025)	–.437 (024)	.066 (253)	–.827 (36)	–.569 (035)	–.023 (253)	–.763 (036)	–.591 (033)
–.003 (256)	–.570 (035)	–.041 (034)	.038 (250)	–.761 (029)	–.373 (027)	–.136 (262)	–.567 (37)	.757 (033)	.069 (258)	–.569 (036)	.007 (032)

114,126 (r = .246)

.057 (207)	-.242 (062)	.123 (064)
-.149 (196)	-.655 (016)	-.298 (023)
-.095 (193)	-.494 (013)	-.124 (020)

114,134 (r = .758)

.075 (208)	.015 (085)	-.122 (092)
-.096 (193)	-.806 (017)	-.431 (025)
-.100 (197)	-.620 (019)	.672 (022)

114,144 (r = .313)

.053 (204)	-.437 (045)	-.361 (053)
-.124 (193)	-.858 (015)	-.430 (022)
-.041 (197)	-.631 (028)	-.061 (032)

114,157 (r = .076)

-.108 (195)	-.479 (025)	-.211 (029)
-.002 (192)	-.696 (014)	-.334 (022)
.080 (193)	-.749 (020)	-.421 (025)

114,169 (r = .644)

.002 (261)	-.095 (174)	-.069 (180)
.016 (195)	-.864 (028)	-.596 (035)
-.052 (200)	-.371 (030)	.424 (035)

114,170 (r = .338)

-.154 (217)	-.227 (082)	-.191 (090)
.107 (196)	-.756 (026)	-.635 (034)
-.038 (197)	-.522 (029)	.021 (032)

126,134 (r = .330)

.169 (108)	-.179 (086)	-.065 (082)
-.260 (059)	-.889 (013)	-.806 (010)
.179 (059)	-.530 (013)	.009 (011)

126,144 (r = .019)

-.180 (080)	-.322 (040)	-.314 (040)
-.275 (058)	-.808 (011)	-.975 (007)
.207 (063)	-.605 (025)	-.338 (020)

126,157 (r = -.074)

-.178 (063)	-.453 (020)	-.282 (016)
-.222 (056)	-.969 (011)	-.791 (007)
-.089 (058)	-.731 (016)	-.537 (012)

126,169 (r = .289)

-.055 (199)	-.147 (175)	.119 (171)
-.190 (064)	-.933 (025)	-.765 (021)
-.018 (069)	-.060 (025)	.011 (024)

126,170 (r = .122)

-.166 (108)	-.198 (080)	.084 (077)
-.167 (067)	-.796 (023)	-.866 (019)
-.179 (067)	.036 (022)	-.214 (021)

134,144 (r = .272)

-.077 (103)	-.486 (042)	-.316 (042)
-.181 (085)	-.985 (012)	-.474 (012)
.065 (087)	-.609 (025)	-.011 (025)

Table C-3 continued.

134,157 (r = .012)

-.141 (092)	-.442 (021)	-.324 (020)
-.134 (083)	-.983 (011)	-.526 (013)
.112 (084)	-.738 (016)	-.418 (017)

134,169 (r = .793)

-.019 (202)	.074 (173)	-.110 (178)
-.236 (093)	-.939 (025)	-.610 (025)
-.114 (092)	-.409 (027)	.738 (025)

134,170 (r = .254)

-.169 (128)	-.251 (081)	-.209 (083)
-.057 (087)	-.852 (023)	-.642 (026)
-.167 (092)	-.438 (024)	-.043 (022)

144,157 (r = -.052)

-.333 (049)	-.404 (019)	-.369 (030)
-.227 (040)	-.996 (009)	-.464 (021)
-.346 (045)	-.710 (014)	-.442 (025)

144,169 (r = .251)

-.082 (174)	-.026 (179)	-.144 (187)
-.581 (021)	-.696 (035)	-.508 (051)
-.372 (026)	-.125 (035)	-.206 (050)

144,170 (r = .028)

-.310 (099)	-.216 (079)	-.270 (090)
-.416 (051)	-.833 (021)	-.650 (033)
-.334 (049)	-.435 (023)	-.358 (032)

157,169 (r = .053)

.027 (179)	-.092 (172)	-.041 (174)
-.508 (031)	-.812 (021)	-.774 (027)
-.314 (034)	-.364 (025)	-.335 (029)

157,170 (r = .065)

-.116 (087)	-.201 (079)	-.175 (078)
-.520 (031)	-.962 (021)	-.617 (024)
-.352 (030)	-.425 (023)	-.443 (027)

169,170 (r = .329)

.026 (197)	-.241 (088)	-.272 (094)
.061 (175)	-.761 (033)	-.572 (037)
-.135 (183)	-.592 (035)	-.003 (031)

Section C–3

CORRELATIONS BETWEEN EMPLOYMENT ESTIMATES FOR SMSA AND
NON-SMSA SUBDIVISIONS OF FIFTEEN SAMPLE INDUSTRIES

This section explains the data in Table C–4 which were calculated after dividing the estimated employment data for each sample industry into two parts: the first 205 regions, which are all SMSA's or Metropolitan SEA's and the last 172 regions which are OBE economic areas excluding all SMSA's. The SMSA parts of each sample industry were then correlated and the non-SMSA parts were correlated (after omitted paired zero observations). Table C–4 contains three coefficients of correlation and three sample sizes for each of the 105 pairs of industries.

Table C–4. Summary of SMSA-non-SMSA differences in geographic association for 15 industries.

Industry pair	Correlation coefficients (sample sizes)		
	All regions	SMSA regions	Non-SMSA regions
6,47	.729	.763	.208
	(368)	(204)	(164)
6,61	.435	.483	.327
	(369)	(205)	(164)
6,67	.722	.753	.377
	(371)	(204)	(167)
6,70	.751	.761	.519
	(371)	(204)	(167)
6,114	.670	.704	.276
	(369)	(204)	(165)
6,126	.301	.293	.229
	(368)	(204)	(164)
6,134	.593	.606	.254
	(368)	(204)	(164)
6,144	.305	.284	.080
	(368)	(204)	(164)
6,150	.421	.397	.483
	(369)	(204)	(165)
6,157	.062	.128	.218
	(368)	(204)	(164)
6,169	.692	.709	.532
	(370)	(204)	(166)
6,170	.477	.469	.477
	(368)	(204)	(164)
6,178	.531	.553	.016
	(369)	(204)	(165)
6,188	.638	.646	.353
	(368)	(204)	(164)

Table C–4 continued

Industry pair	Correlation coefficients (sample sizes)		
	All regions	SMSA regions	Non-SMSA regions
47,61	.302	.378	−.068
	(189)	(117)	(72)
47,67	.587	.636	−.013
	(258)	(149)	(109)
47,70	.825	.856	.191
	(293)	(168)	(125)
47,114	.698	.745	.104
	(240)	(146)	(94)
47,126	.268	.263	.039
	(141)	(93)	(48)
47,134	.749	.772	−.008
	(145)	(95)	(50)
47,144	.253	.238	.100
	(135)	(88)	(47)
47,150	.249	.249	.083
	(176)	(106)	(70)
47,157	.026	.154	.053
	(129)	(80)	(49)
47,169	.777	.815	.264
	(238)	(140)	(98)
47,170	.418	.448	−.023
	(169)	(111)	(58)
47,178	.441	.465	−.220
	(144)	(88)	(56)
47,188	.567	.577	−.146
	(199)	(121)	(78)
61,67	.281	.316	.156
	(262)	(152)	(110)
61,70	.321	.346	.300
	(299)	(171)	(128)
61,114	.327	.404	.022
	(243)	(146)	(97)
61,126	.058	.066	.034
	(157)	(99)	(58)
61,134	.138	.176	−.117
	(171)	(110)	(61)
61,144	−.064	−.078	−.104
	(155)	(96)	(59)
61,150	.160	.117	.314
	(180)	(109)	(71)
61,167	−.041	.014	−.071
	(145)	(87)	(58)
61,169	.216	.219	.229
	(238)	(139)	(99)
61,170	.430	.479	.283
	(180)	(114)	(66)
61,178	.061	.081	−.125
	(161)	(92)	(69)
61,188	.497	.597	−.080
	(206)	(123)	(83)
67,70	.673	.706	.256
	(315)	(176)	(139)

Table C–4 continued

Industry pair	Correlation coefficients (sample sizes)		
	All regions	SMSA regions	Non-SMSA regions
67,114	.535	.593	.004
	(287)	(166)	(121)
67,126	.221	.220	−.039
	(246)	(146)	(100)
67,134	.548	.575	.112
	(252)	(151)	(101)
67,144	.180	.166	−.075
	(238)	(140)	(98)
67,150	.264	.262	.124
	(252)	(146)	(106)
67,157	−.015	.054	−.014
	(243)	(140)	(103)
67,169	.619	.668	.170
	(282)	(162)	(120)
67,170	.268	.272	.129
	(259)	(154)	(105)
67,178	.345	.363	−.055
	(247)	(140)	(107)
67,188	.513	.534	−.026
	(271)	(154)	(117)
70,114	.767	.811	.181
	(304)	(177)	(127)
70,126	.353	.348	.305
	(292)	(169)	(123)
70,134	.866	.882	.344
	(290)	(167)	(123)
70,144	.351	.343	.014
	(291)	(168)	(123)
70,150	.347	.327	.472
	(296)	(171)	(125)
70,157	.071	.159	.208
	(290)	(167)	(123)
70,169	.865	.891	.547
	(312)	(178)	(134)
70,170	.348	.335	.418
	(295)	(173)	(122)
70,178	.401	.414	−.092
	(294)	(166)	(128)
70,188	.563	.564	.186
	(302)	(172)	(130)
114,126	.246	.248	.106
	(228)	(140)	(88)
114,134	.758	.802	.054
	(224)	(137)	(87)
114,144	.313	.319	−.045
	(229)	(140)	(89)
114,150	.277	.290	.081
	(236)	(140)	(96)
114,157	.076	.194	.116
	(221)	(136)	(85)
114,169	.644	.699	.106
	(278)	(162)	(116)

Studies in applied regional science

Vol. 1
On the use of input-output models for regional planning
W. A. Schaffer.

This volume is devoted to the use of input-output techniques in regional planning. The study provides a clear introduction to the essential ideas of input-output analysis. Particular emphasis is placed on the intricate problems of data collection at a regional level.
Attention is focused on the applicability of input-output analysis in the field of regional planning. Alternative methods such as shift-and-share techniques are discussed. For means of clear illustration an extensive regional study of the Georgia economy has been capably employed.

ISBN 90 207 0626 8

Vol. 2
Forecasting transportation impacts upon land use
P. F. Wendt.

This reader concentrates on transportation problems in urban areas. After a survey of model techniques for analyzing transportation and land use problems, several new methods in the field of transportation and land-use planning (including Delphi-methods and interaction models) are developed. In the study particular attention is paid to forecasting techniques for regional-urban developments. The book is exemplified by an extensive set of applied methods in transportation land-use planning for the Georgia region.

ISBN 90 207 0627 6

Martinus Nijhoff Social Sciences Division Leiden 1976

Vol. 3
Estimation of stochastic input-output models
S. D. Gerking

The primary objective of this monograph is to develop a method for measuring the uncertainty in estimates of the technical coefficients in an input-output model. Specifically, it is demonstrated that if two-stage least squares is used to estimate these parameters, then uncertainty may be judged according to the magnitude of the standard errors of these estimates.
This study also describes three further applications of the two-stage least squares estimation technique in an input-output context. The techniques and applications are illustrated using cross-sectional input-output data from West Virginia.

ISBN 90 207 0628 4

Vol. 4
Locational behavior in manufacturing industries
William R. Latham III

Agglomerative economies form a central concept in regional science. Yet an empirical determination of agglomeration advantages has been minimal up to now. To help remedy the situation, this study contains an effort to gauge the order of magnitude of agglomeration advantages, based on a careful inspection of industrial location data. The determinants of geographic association behavior by individual industry are carefully analysed.
A statistical test shows that general agglomerative economies are significant factors for industrial location behavior. The result of the study, and the policy conclusions it would seem to justify, are presented; moreover, ways of extending and improving the analysis are suggested.

ISBN 90 207 0638 1

Vol. 5
Regional economic structure and environmental pollution
B.E.M.G. Coupé
This book deals with the ever-increasing problem of
pollution. The author has constructed an extensive
interregional model for economic activities and pollution.
Each region has its own internal structure, expressed by
means of intersectoral commodity flows, investments,
employment, consumption and pollution. In addition,
interregional linkages are taken into account.
Coupé's two-region model (applied to some Dutch
provinces) is used to calculate an equilibrium in terms
of production and pollution abatement. The solution
procedure is based on a programming model. The model
aims at supplying a means of fighting pollution and
managing the environment, with a view to guiding the
regions to an acceptable life level.

ISBN 90 207 0646 2

Vol. 6
The demand for urban water
P. Darr, S. L. Feldman, C. Kamen
Because the urban water industry remained relatively
impervious to general inflationary trends until the early
1970's tariff design and water demand forecasting played
a relatively minor role in utility management. General
shortages in supply were often abetted by capacity
additions designed using common engineering practice.
However, the range of choice for water management can
include adjustments to remedy disequilibria through
management of the demand side of the market.
This volume explores the components affecting demands
using combined economic, engineering and social
psychological tools and recommends remedies in tariff
design to conform to basic economic postulates.

ISBN 90 207 0647 0

28. 5 0